Dear God ...
Dear George ...

By the same Author

SO GOD SAID TO ME . . .

RICHARD ADAMS

Dear God...
Dear George...

Drawings by
FRANK FINCH

LONDON
EPWORTH PRESS

7162 0348 0

Enquiries should be addressed to
The Methodist Publishing House
Wellington Road
Wimbledon
London SW19 8EU
Printed in Great Britain by
Ebenezer Baylis and Son Ltd,
The Trinity Press, Worcester, and London

Contents

To put you in the picture . . .

George Wilson would say that there was once a time when 'sin' was a word that came readily to the lips of Hot Gospel preachers who would, perhaps with un-Christian relish, condemn the sinners of their congregations to everlasting torment in the flames of hell-fire. But not any more. The old 'Bible-thumpers' frequently envisaged these agonies consuming the drunkard and wife-beater, and the harlot. Today, were sin conspicuous at all, George would reckon it to be conspicuous by its absence. What has happened to the preacher's fire and call to repentance, the emotional appeal resulting in the dramatic conversion so essential for the sinner's return to Christ, and his only means of salvation and respectability?

George, being a respectable family man himself, newly moved into a small village from which he commutes daily to the city, where he finds his calling as a local preacher somewhat at odds with his employment in an advertising agency, fell to reflecting on the nature of sin. He wondered, if the Seven Deadly Sins still existed, what they were, and whether he was guilty of any of them. It was in this frame of mind that he only needed the chance remark of a neighbour to cause him to conduct a most unusual correspondence. . . .

Sin . . . and a glass of pale ale

Dear God,

I went to visit Maudie today. Jack Williams has brought her bed downstairs. When I went in, she was sitting up in it, her thin white hair uncombed, her shiny, wrinkled hands intertwined across the turned-down sheet. I wondered if she knew she was dying.

You know Maudie well. Better than I do, certainly; but she made a remark today that set me thinking, so I just thought I'd drop you a line. It can't be much of a life for her at eighty-four, living alone at the end of that bleak row of council houses, with only a cold tap in the kitchen and a heap of wet coal by the back door. She must be lonely, God, though many of the villagers would say that was her own fault, that it was her cantankerous nature and sharp tongue that had put up the barriers to any sympathy they might have had for her. You know that we haven't been in the village long, so we tried to take her as we found her, assuming that poor, unmarried Maudie is simply frustrated and misunderstood.

Does she know that she's dying of cancer? You'll have heard her tell me today that she feels she's daily growing weaker. She can't bring herself to eat a proper meal, yet she kept saying, over and over again, 'I do need something nourishing, something nourishing.' Her face was pale, her lips were dry. The enriched protein powdered food I mixed up for her in some warm milk seemed thick, she said, and tasteless. She said she fancied something sharp.

Trouble with Maudie is, she belongs to a strict Primitive Methodist tradition. You know what I mean, God. The very words produce in my mind a picture of starched collars with faces to match. They stressed the evils of alcohol and advocated total abstinence. Drink was liquid sin.

I didn't notice the empty bottle and the used glass when I first arrived. When Maudie saw that I'd spotted them standing on the table, a combination of guilt and embarrassment brought a little colour to her cheeks for once.

It was Jack Williams, of course, who had taken pity on her. A regular caller at the *Hastings Arms*, is Jack. I thought it was rather touching that, in his own way, he'd thought to bring Maudie a little cheer and comfort. She'd wanted something sharp, so he'd brought her a bottle of pale ale.

'Jack Williams brought me that,' she said to me, rather apologetically, 'I expect you think I'm a wicked woman.'

You know, God, that I didn't think anything of the sort, and that I told her so, but I can't be sure that she believed me. The tradition of sin and shame associated with the 'bottle' which her brand of Christianity has imposed upon her is too strong for any words of mine to bring release or a feeling of forgiveness.

You must let me know if I was wrong, God, but I didn't feel that forgiveness was even called for. It seemed to me that Maudie had humbly accepted a gift from a neighbour who had showed his compassion in a way that to him seemed natural and right. I reckon that at a time when Maudie's life lacks any kind of flavour, to taste the sharpness of a glass of pale ale is probably the least sin she could have committed.

It was when I got home, God, that I wondered if you considered it to be a sin. I sometimes think you would simply smile at some of the things we feel guilty about. Being human, I suppose we've a tendency to get things all out of proportion, often magnifying the little misdemeanours, so as to avoid facing the really major issues.

The more I thought about it, the more uncertain I became as to what sin was. Amongst this clutter of books on my desk, there's one that defines sin as any action that separates us from you. I suppose it would have to be a *deliberate* action, wouldn't it? You wouldn't class errors as sins, would you? I'd like to believe that honest mistakes, errors of judgement, good intentions upset by circumstances, while confirming the frailty and fallibility of human nature, are not necessarily sins. I mean – don't we *need* human error to prevent us from getting ideas above our station?

Trouble is, that could give us just the excuse we need to go on sinning.

If you can spare the time to reply, I'd appreciate some clarification. Does the judgement of an action as a sin depend, like Maudie's glass of ale, on circumstances? Certainly, life would be a lot simpler if you could issue a fully comprehensive list of sins which we could then strive assiduously to avoid. I can't help feeling sometimes that you deliberately make life difficult for us by allowing commendable activities to hover dangerously on the edge of sin's domain. No wonder so many people topple in. What cunning ruse is this, God? Are you so anxious to demonstrate your generous spirit of forgiveness that you need a few of us to commit the occasional sin? Maybe the more we wallow in sin, the more glory you can attach to yourself for stooping so low to redeem us!

Oh dear! Now I suppose I've gone too far. Sorry, God, but you do understand how confusing it all is? Is it irony or paradox or both that allows me to think that sin is something that cuts me off from you, while those marvellous words from Paul's letter to the Romans sing like music in my head, the promise that I dare not disbelieve – 'I am sure that neither death, nor life, nor angels, nor principalities, nor things present, nor things to come, nor powers, nor height, nor depth, nor anything else in all creation, will be able to separate us from the love of God in Christ Jesus our Lord'?

What *am* I to believe, God? That sin is as much a part of creation as love, deliberately put there by you, so that we may learn how to fight the one and embrace the other? It is tempting to think that freedom of choice is as malicious as it is generous. My dilemma gets worse!

For my sake and yours, God, write back soon.

Yours sincerely,

George

... and a clatter of saucepans

Dear God,

You'll have to forgive the tone of this letter, God, but I'm hopping mad and it's bound to show.

How can anyone behave the way that man does? You'll know who I mean, God. That tall, thin-faced, mean-mannered git Edward Morris with the drooping moustache, and the inquisitorial metal-framed spectacles.

Who *does* he think he is? He came into my office this morning and delivered a monologue about efficiency and dedication to the job that was hardly designed to improve mine – though *he* clearly thought it would. I wanted to tell him what he could do with his job there and then! It's not as though he's had the experience that I've had. Well, *you* know, God, if anyone does. I've come up the hard way, working my way up from office boy to senior management, learning the job by doing it. I didn't come in by the side door just because I'd got a degree in sociology and happened to marry the managing director's daughter.

Sociology! You'd think he'd *know* how to handle people!

You know him, don't you, God? You know *his* trouble. He suffers from an inferiority that's not so much a complex as a malignant disease, and strives to boost his withered ego by criticizing others and belittling efforts he wouldn't know how to begin to make himself. How *dare* he criticize me?

You must allow me, God, at least a *little* righteous indignation. I wouldn't admit to hating him exactly, but who would blame me if I did? Soft-tongued he is, and lily-livered; his bravado only gains its strength like a parasite by exploiting the weaknesses of others, sucking at their wounds, licking his lips in anticipation of their downfall.

If *only* I could answer him back! But you know I'm never any good in an argument. I took great care preparing those papers he so gleefully threw back at me this morning; corrected every detail, re-typed them. But he can't agree, he says in his woolly text-book jargon, with the 'underlying philosophy'.

You *tell* him, God. You know as well as I do. *Philosophy* never sold a tin of biscuits, never mind launched an entire advertising campaign. Flair and imagination, that's what matters, and he's got neither. Philosophy! I ask you!

But it's all very well to write this down now. Why couldn't you have given me the words this morning when I needed them? I just sat there taking a verbal battering, without a whisper in my own defence – well, nothing that made me feel any better anyway. I *love* the job, God; that's what makes it hurt so when he has the nerve to question my ability and dedication.

It wouldn't be so bad if I could muster up a little respect

for his opinions, but even if he was right, his personality and attitude would be against him. So negative. So full of anxiety about the failures of other people. So sure it's everyone else who's responsible for all that's wrong with the world. And he thinks *he* can put everything right overnight by picking on a single individual.

He's so smooth and condescending – 'It's quality of vision that's important, don't you think Mr. W.? Perception, tenacity and commitment, Mr. W., the only way to maintain the highest standards, wouldn't you say?'

Did you hear him say that, God? Did you hear the super-cilious *******? – no, I'd better not write what I thought! Forgive me.

But why *me*? That's what I'd like to know. You know me, God. I do my best, don't I? I know I'm not perfect. I make mistakes like anyone else. But it makes me so *angry*. Only you know *how* angry, when lofty Edward – yes, Edward, not even plain Ted – snooty-nosed Edward Morris makes out that he knows so much better!

One of life's back-seat drivers, that's what he is. Put *him* in the driving seat and we'd soon be in the ditch, but as long as he sits in the back, he thinks he can carp and comment, deceiving himself that no one knows better than he. The juice on which such men thrive is criticism and complaint. He watches life from the touchline, jeering and cat-calling, knowing nothing of the game because, if the truth is known, he's never had the guts to play it like a man.

It's so unfair, God! And I hate injustice, and I hate. . . . Do I hate Edward Morris? I'm too angry to be honest with myself, God. Only you know what my real feelings are, and only you can tell me what to do. Shall I eat humble pie and revise those papers according to his fancy notions? Or shall I tell him what I think of his ideas and offer mine again – tactfully supporting them with hints at my greater knowledge and experience? Or shall I tell him, if that's how he feels, he can stuff the papers – and the job?

I know what you'll say, God. You've said it so often before. Love your enemies. Do good to them that despitefully use you. That's all very well, but this man strains the limits of my tolerance. To think of him as the object of my love and sympathy is to contemplate valuable compassion wasted.

If you were in my shoes you wouldn't find it so easy to forgive and forget, to take it on the chin without thoughts of revenge, or at least some form of retaliation . . . I'm sorry, God. Easy or not, I know you'd do it just the same. But it isn't easy for me. I resent his arrogance. It's enough to make *anyone* fume – though I admit I feel a little less angry for having got it off my chest. But what's to be done? He'll be waiting for an answer at the end of the week. There's time to let the fire die or stoke the furnace so fiercely that Edward Morris withers in the heat. How gladly would I see him wither!

Write soon,
Yours sincerely,
George

P.S. Forgot to mention that Maudie was angry with *me* today. I suppose you heard anyway, but I have to confess to being tactless. She was complaining, as is her habit now and again, about the terrible way village folks have treated her, and how no one bothers to visit her now she can't get out. I ventured to suggest – to her with the utmost delicacy, of course, though I put it a shade more bluntly to you – that she might well be getting only what she deserved, considering the number of people who'd felt the sharp edge of her tongue.

It was my turn to feel it then. She said I was no better than the rest of them. What's to be done, God, when honesty provokes cross words? Is truth to be stifled for the sake of peace?

Dear George,

It was good to hear from you again after such a long time, but you really must stop using the office notepaper. It's not honest, you know, and apart from that, I get curious looks from the others in this department who wonder what business I can possibly be conducting with Waverley Advertising. Getting myself a new image perhaps?

Anyway, to deal with the matter you wrote about. I really enjoyed your letter. You know, you should get angry more often; it makes your writing so eloquent. You clearly think it a pity that you find yourself incapable of waxing more eloquent when you're actually faced with your opponent in the office. I would say that you do well to keep quiet. Indeed, I commend your self-restraint. That's half-way to loving your enemies! The other half is to stop regarding him as your opponent. After all, the welfare and – dare I say? – profits of Waverley Advertising rest in both your hands. Why not build the Company's future together?

I know that to admit that the other fellow may be right seems like weakness, but try to regard it as strength. Be generous. Offer to consider his ideas. Offer him the benefit of your experience too, but don't pretend that your way is superior, or in some other way clearly preferable to his. Given the opportunity to discuss it thoroughly, without rancour, he may come to see it your way anyhow. Or you may discover some previously unnoticed merit in his!

You were angry because he wouldn't give in to you. You won't admit that of course. You were not only convinced that your plans were better than his, but you despised his condescending attitude. In fact, you displayed in your letter such expertise in dissecting his character I wonder you don't become a professional psychologist!

Doesn't it occur to you, George, that the weaknesses you single out are more deserving of your sympathy than your anger? If he's so inadequate that he needs to boost his ego by trampling on yours, can't you find a way of giving him confidence? What about treating his ideas seriously, for instance, instead of dismissing them out of hand simply because you can't bring yourself to like the man?

Get beyond that bespectacled mask of his to the man underneath, desperate like you are for recognition and assurance. It would be interesting to know whether or not the faults you see in him are so readily apparent to you because they reflect your own failings. Somewhere, George, there must be a point where his theory and your practicality can meet and produce a worthwhile scheme.

Anger is so rarely productive. Few people have the strength of character and intellect to control anger so that it lends power to valid argument. Mostly, anger takes control of people, breeding irrational and often incoherent thoughts. Some say they can't help losing their tempers, it's just the way they're made. Quite true. After all, I allowed man to develop from the animals who still hunt each other and fight to the death to defend their own territory. It's only natural. You too become angry as a means of defence, protecting your personal opinions and prejudices. One day, when mankind reaches full maturity, I shall expect him to have grown out of such instinctive behaviour, further away from the animals than he is now.

Yes, George. *One day!* Did you think you had reached maturity already? Believe me, you've a long way to go yet!

What really makes people angry is their inability to see their way through a difficulty. Frustration. A voice raised in anger is a cry for help, an unconscious plea for reassurance.

The trouble with your adopted spinster Maudie, is the lack of opportunity she's had for sharing. Sharing is an experience which you, with a wife and two children to think about constantly, have absorbed into your behaviour patterns so unconsciously that you take it for granted – though even you find it easier to be selfish at times. No wonder that Maudie, living alone, finds giving and receiving an embarrassment. She's cultivated a necessary independence which makes it hard for her to admit the need for a helping hand now that illness is making her frail and less capable of doing everything for herself; and her anger is only a natural defence against those offers of assistance she chooses to interpret as interference, no matter how well-intentioned.

Maudie likes to think, as you do, that she knows what's best for her. Advice or home-truths are bound to be hard for her to take. You should have been ready for her hackles to rise, and I'm sure you'll tread more warily next time.

You will have to make allowances for Maudie, but, I'm happy to tell you that your remark, though swiftly rebuked when you made it, has given Maudie some cause for reflection as she lies in bed with little else to do. She would dearly love to feel that she could belong more fully to the life and warmth of the village, and envies you your warm home and family. You could do something, or say something to reassure her, George. It needn't be too late for Maudie.

By the way, George, do you still have trouble with that blue-lidded saucepan? After that day when you found Rosemary at the sink up to her wrists in suds, spasmodically flinging saucepans at the kitchen floor, the one with the blue lid was never quite the same again. The lid wouldn't fit, and it wobbled when you put it on the cooker. You hadn't been married long. I knew why she was angry, but it took *you* completely by surprise. I remember your look of bewilderment as another saucepan hit the floor and skidded across the tiles. You don't remember what the quarrel was about even now, do you? But I know you'll never forget the agony of it; the painful silences when neither of you knew what to say to heal the wounds. And when, at last, you ventured to speak, the tears you both shed, and the tentative, desperate embraces, and finally, the deeper understanding of each other's love which distress and reconciliation made possible.

You see, George, I have at least built something positive into the nature of anger, for when the heat of it has subsided there is always the possibility of reconciliation. The mental and physical struggle provides the friction by which two human beings are afterwards fused more closely together, their very quarrelling a demonstration of their need for each other.

Isn't it a paradox that anger, which seems to alienate one person from another, is really an expression of the need to give and receive love? Just for a while, there has been a barrier erected, preventing communication and under-standing. So I ask you to remain open and vulnerable, ready to receive the thoughtless or deliberate malice that comes your way, absorbing and neutralising it by the power of your silence, winning the battle by refusing to arm yourself with the weapons of vindictiveness and self-justification.

That doesn't mean being soft, George. It means being resilient. And if you think that vulnerability and resilience do not go hand in hand, then I must ask you to consider seriously your membership of the Christian Church.

I had a son who was both vulnerable and resilient, and from that strange mixture came the joy of resurrection and reconciliation. I'm sure you know the story, but you may find it worthwhile to re-read it.

In the meantime, I wish you well in your discussions with Edward Morris. Give him my kind regards.

Yours sincerely,
God

P.S. Looking again at your letter, I don't seem to have properly answered the questions you asked at the end, but I'm sure you'll manage all right.

G.

. . . and treasure on earth

Dear God,

This will surprise you – a thank you letter. I don't suppose you get very many of those, so here am I restoring the balance a little.

I want to thank you for the tremendous good fortune you've sent my way during the last few months. It was certainly confirmation of the old saying that God moves in a mysterious way. You certainly do, or perhaps a better word would be 'incredible'. Certainly it was unexpected. Who would have thought that Edward Morris, of all people, would have given *me* the chance to earn some extra cash? I suppose he's not such a bad chap really. We all have our off-days, after all. Even me.

Anyway – you'll know that he was approached by some people from Eastward Television who wanted to make a series of programmes about the advertising business – a sort of soap-opera about soap-selling! It seems they needed a consultant, well-versed in the intricacies and dealings of the advertising world, so that they could be certain of getting the script and visual details right.

I must give credit where it's due. Edward Morris actually admitted that he was a comparative newcomer to the business and more of an administrator and organizer on the personnel side of things than your real creative media-man – at least, that's what he told me he'd told them – and if they were really looking for someone who knew advertising inside out, they should get in touch with me.

So they did. They took me out to lunch so that we could discuss what they wanted me to do and agree on a suitable fee for my services. The lunch was magnificent and left me gasping, but the fee was the best part. Maybe I've been living in a dream world where I've simply accepted that money is inevitably in short supply. Perhaps they've got the right idea about appropriate remuneration for what a man does. Who's to say what anyone is worth?

The blow came, when I remembered I'd have to pay tax on it all. I hadn't realized before just what a large slice of my salary went in tax. I'd always glanced rather quickly at my pay-slip, felt grateful for the final total, and not given a great deal of thought to how much had been deducted. What you haven't had, you don't miss, I suppose. When the cheques from EWTV had amounted to nearly a thousand pounds, the thought of parting with over three hundred of it to the Inland Revenue was horrifying. I mean, I'd *earned* that three hundred quid!

However, the tax-man didn't seem to be in any great hurry for it, so while I was waiting for his Notice of Assessment, I put it in the Building Society and let it accumulate some interest.

In the meantime, Rosemary and I had such fun spending the balance. No, that's not quite true. After the delight of signing the first few, seemingly extravagant cheques, the pleasure was strangely clouded by an air of disenchantment. We *did* enjoy spending the money, but it would only have been real *fun* if it had been limitless – which, of course, it wasn't. We soon came to the end of it, and sometimes we hardly dare part with the money because we couldn't be absolutely certain we were spending it on what we really wanted. To have the money in the bank was a comfortable feeling. Signing cheques for large amounts was frightening and painful. I began to wonder if you hadn't had a hand in it somewhere, deliberately turning the milk of affluence sour, but I suppose we only wanted to have our cake and eat it as well.

Mind you, God, I wouldn't mind sampling the high life just for a while to see what it's like. I mean, there can't be that much harm in money and possessions. I know what Jesus said about it being easier for a camel to get through the eye of a needle than for a rich man to enter the kingdom of God – but he didn't say it couldn't be done, did he? I'd quite like the chance to prove that it can.

Surely, someone has to have more while others have less. How else can there be opportunity for compassion, for giving and receiving? And what of sacrifice? Is it to become obsolete? Or are we to expect that those who have plenty shall give so generously to those who have little or nothing, that the rich themselves become poor and the roles are reversed? Your set-up down here on earth confuses me, God. It's almost as though you were content for there to be haves and have-nots in order to make generosity a continual possibility. Love thriving on the existence of poverty and need? It doesn't make sense.

As I write, the annual round of wage demands, go-slows and strikes is just beginning again – the winter of industrial discontent. I have to keep a daily check on the central-heating oil. It's getting low, and the tanker drivers are on strike. The lorry-drivers are on strike as well. Rosemary came back from the shops today with the news that there are no fresh vegetables. If I can't get any petrol at the garage tomorrow, I'm not sure that I shall be able to get into work. There won't be any buses because the bus companies are running out of fuel too.

The workers want more money. Don't we all? Some of them believe they've a right to demand it, if only to bring their pay-packets up to the level of others doing similar or identical jobs in other parts of the country. Parity, I think they call it. I don't suppose I can quarrel with them if they say 'It's only fair!' The whole question hinges on the concept of justice. It's only fair that a man should have enough to eat, enough money to pay for a roof over his head, and to clothe his children. If only we could all agree on what was an adequate standard of living.

But I rather suspect that if we all had the same – if there was a sudden standstill in the acquisition of money, goods and property, while it was all shared out equally, it wouldn't be long before those with ambition and intelligence had secured more than their fair share by taking advantage of the less able. Even so, the less able would *expect* to pay for the goods and services the others would supply. Is that fair or not, God? Is it exploitation, or simply making use of our talents and reaping a suitable reward for doing so?

That parable Jesus told about the three men who were entrusted with a sum of money while their employer went away, worries me, God. When the one who made the most of his investments (which I assume, at some stage, must have inevitably been at someone else's expense), was Jesus condoning the practice of getting something for nothing?

When people go on strike, my immediate reaction is to accuse them of greed, especially when their industrial action puts the general public at risk or deprives them of necessities. I would never have thought I was a greedy man, but I have to admit that the temporary riches that Rosemary and I enjoyed *did* make us long for more. Now that it's all spent we're getting used to the standing-still existence again. There's not much point in going on strike in my line of business. Secretly, if I'm really honest, I suspect that the world might get along quite well without advertising men vigorously persuading people to buy things they never wanted in the first place. But don't let Edward Morris know I've said that!

That reminds me of the other opportunity that came my way while I was visiting Eastward Television's Studios. I was asked – as, of course, you know – to take part in a studio discussion on the morality of advertising, in their late-night religious programme 'God Alone Knows'. You do make life interesting for me. Lights, cameras, make-up, and all the technical wizardry – I find it fascinating. Thanks again. You heard me, no doubt, telling the other members of the discussion group how dependent everyone's welfare is on a flourishing economy, to which the advertising industry makes no small contribution.

Edward Morris saw the programme when it was transmitted and congratulated me most warmly on that. He seemed a little embarrassed when he realized he'd been almost glowing in his remarks. I think he may even have been a little bit jealous. Still, I do seem to have some merit in his eyes at last. Perhaps it was simply a matter of giving him time to get to know me – and me him, of course. I'm beginning to feel I can forgive him for that first caustic encounter. The wounds will heal, given time.

By the way, God, you seem rather slow to do anything about that other opportunity I hoped would have begun to come my way before now. You know I mentioned to the Programme Controller at EWTV that I do the odd bit of writing in my spare time, and asked if it would be worth my while to submit a few scripts. I've got several ideas which I'm sure would make first-rate TV programmes.

You never reveal the future to us, do you? I wish you

would sometimes. I'd like to be certain about the wisdom or folly of throwing up Waverley Advertising and plunging into full-time writing. I know it's early days yet, but after the excitement of the TV studio and the pleasant, stimulating company I found myself in, I suddenly realized how cut off I had been from the real world. Once we had made our programme, we retired to the viewing room upstairs to await the playback so that we could judge our performances. While we waited, the whiskies, vodkas, camparis and sodas flowed freely – all at Eastward's expense, naturally. The atmosphere was so relaxed and congenial. They certainly know how to do things in style.

Suddenly, the work here in my dismal office seemed so dull and routine. I'm not an ambitious man, as you know, but I'm sure there must be a more exhilarating and creative way of earning a living, not to say more remunerative. It's not that I desperately want the money, of course, but the change would be good for me, don't you think? The money, of course, is always welcome, but one of the points I had to concede in the studio discussion was that TV advertising encourages greed, and I suppose nowhere more blatantly than in the slogan the banks use to sell their credit card facilities – 'Have it when you want it. Pay when you can.' I'm glad it wasn't anyone at Waverley Advertising that dreamed that one up.

I sat in church the other day, thinking about that slogan. (The sermon was especially dreary. If I hadn't been occupied with my own thoughts I might have dropped off to sleep.) I got to wondering why advertising comes in for so much criticism from preachers and sociologists. On the whole – that terrible banks commercial apart, we only present people with a message that says the product is available, possibly adding a little information about it. That's no sin, is it? They're under no pressure or obligation to buy or do anything the advertisements recommend.

What I'm taking a long time to get around to, God, is that

24

I actually sat there wondering if I was covetous. Rosemary and I have always been more or less content with what we've got. If the money hasn't been available, we've gone without. If we were really covetous – really deep-down greedy – I'm sure we'd go to any lengths to satisfy our wants, even if it meant neglecting our health, or the children, stealing or murder. That's when it becomes evil, isn't it. I'm glad I'm not like that.

I even have slightly guilty feelings about something Maudie said the other day. She doesn't seem to be getting any better, God. She called in her solicitor to make some changes in her will, and I rather suspect she's made some arrangements in my favour. I *do* hope not. I shall feel so guilty if, after she's dead, a cheque arrives from her solicitors, simply because I've tried to provide a little company and comfort in her last few months. There must be a host of people in the village who've shown her kindnesses over the years, to say nothing of their patience and tolerance. I've hardly been in the village five minutes. It's so unfair. I shall feel as though I've stealthily contrived a little windfall for myself.

And its not only Maudie. So many people seem unable to accept a favour. They *must* offer payment. I ran Mrs Spooner into the city last week to visit her husband in hospital. She hasn't a car so I knew she'd appreciate a lift. I didn't want any payment, as you know. I wanted to go into the library anyway, and I didn't have to hang about for too long afterwards. Knowing that I wouldn't accept anything for myself, what did she do? Turned up at the house next day with two boxes of chocolates – 'for the kiddies'.

It may not exactly encourage covetousness, God, but I'm worried, for your sake, that small gestures like this may be the thin end of a wedge that ultimately pushes open a gap that lets wholesale greed into the world on a glorious rampage. The attitude of too many, spoken and unspoken, is 'What's in it for me?'

Oh dear, I do ramble on, don't I? If I write scripts for TV the way I write letters, I shan't get anything accepted. Trouble is, once I get going, one thought leads to another and there you are. Still, this is just between you and me, isn't it, and at least I'm ending on a thankful note, which is what I set out to do. To have enough and to be content with what I've got is a source of great security and satisfaction.

Thanks again,
Yours sincerely,
George

Dear George,

Fancy you thinking that a thank-you letter would surprise.
You know better than that. Besides, I get more of them than
you might think, though that doesn't mean I'm not pleased
to receive one. I was glad to have yours, especially after such
a long time, but then, I know how busy you've been with
your extra commitments in television. I'd expected you
would take some pleasure in extending your talents. I'm
pleased to see you making the most of the opportunities
I've put your way, though I've also noticed how disen-
chanted you've become with your job at Waverley Advertising. However, you must accept the rough with the smooth,
you know. If you go on longing, as you are now, for the
life of ease and luxury you seem to think working perma-
nently for television would provide you'll become even more
disgruntled. In any case, your dissatisfaction at Waverley
has more to do with the proximity of Edward Morris than
with any real loss of interest in the job itself. Don't think
you can deceive me into thinking that all is now sweetness
and light between you. Your remarks speak more potently
of condescension than forgiveness towards him.

However, you clearly seem to be in a state of moral confusion over all the money you've suddenly found yourself
with, so I'd better assist your thinking on the matter if I can.
After all, money is something you humans invented just to
make your transactions a little more manageable; it's not as
though it's really worth anything. It's only out of sympathy
for your bewilderment that I have anything to do with it
at all. What seems to be worrying you most, George – and
I commend the sensitivity that promotes it – is the possession
of so much when others have so little. You feel guilty at

having such an unfair advantage over the poor. You have, again commendably, forgotten that compared to the richest men in your world, what you regard as riches is a mere pittance. From me, I suppose you'll think that's dangerous talk. You'll begin to think that you've only to grow a thick skin against the deprivations of other people and you can shed the feelings of guilt they cause in you. Insensitivity, George, is half-way to committing most sins. Covetousness is really nothing to do with whether you have more or less than other people, but with how the desire to have something affects you as a person, both in your relationship with me and with others.

Many people use money wisely, but I've often seen money use people, directing their actions, or worse, preventing them from seeing what their real motives are for what they do. For instance: too lazy to look for any better measure of human worth, you use money and possessions as an indicator of success or failure. Finding no satisfaction in work, you look to money for compensation. How it blinds you to reality, George! I *know* – you've always thought money and possessions *were* reality, and that such things as job satisfaction or spiritual well-being were of the imagination. When will you learn that in my kingdom it is wealth that is illusory?

The peculiar phenomenon you call inflation is the greatest evidence for this. You are for ever increasing the speed with which you chase after more money, only to find that you remain in the same place. The reality is that the more you earn the less it's worth. By contrast, the tiniest portion of spiritual riches has value beyond price. The merest glimpse of the joy it brings is like the pearl of great price for which the man in Jesus' parable sold all he had in order to buy it.

What I'm really saying is that your shortsightedness causes you to operate a strange system of rewarding men according to the talents they have or the responsibility they carry. It often seems to me that the higher people are promoted the less work they do and the more they get paid for doing it. They're *supposed* to be carrying more responsibility than anyone else; very often they are furthest from responsibility. How easy it is for them, when they receive a complaint, to blame it on the stupidity of those beneath them. They're no better than the man on the shop floor excusing his own carelessness by inventing grievances to lay at the door of those in authority over him.

If I am digressing a little it is because there is so much to say on this matter, and mainly because the sins of your fathers are visiting you in your own generation. It is hard to turn back history, and I know only too well what happens to men who try. They are labelled as cranks and idealists who need to be put away or destroyed. They are deemed out of touch with reality, when in truth they are the only ones who have any grasp of it. Some have been stoned or crucified because the general public has not been able to match their vision and courage, and has allowed the mistakes of history to continue to flow over them like an unstoppable flood.

I am referring, of course, to the unequal distribution of wealth which you accept as inevitable, and which, while you say you deplore it, you seek to perpetuate with wage differentials. Is it really right to pay a man a salary which has been determined by the value society places on the contribution he makes to the economy? Profit and loss can be easily counted, but they are no measure of a people's contribution to each other as *people*. Care and compassion cannot be worked out on a pocket calculator. While the company director bellows 'Time is money', and employs time and motion experts to improve efficiency, he is failing to recognize that people do not stop being people just because they've clocked on at 7.30 in the morning.

And why do you think it fair to pay a man more because he has exceptional talents? If I have given him gifts above those of the average man, then he should not only be grateful, but recognize that what he does comes easily and naturally to him, and is therefore of no special merit. Why should he expect to be paid more for putting to use something which came to him as a free gift?

I will take the dangerous step of using an illustration from your present industrial unrest – dangerous, because I will have to use your terms and label people as you tend to label them. For some strange reason, you rate a dustman in a category significantly lower than that, say, of a bank manager; yet what an outcry there is when the dustmen go on strike and health-endangering rubbish starts to accumulate in the streets. Suddenly perspectives change. Sadly they return to their normal state of myopia when the crisis is over.

The one question that your letter really asks is whether people are deprived by other men's riches. Let me ask *you* a question by way of reply. Would anyone else *really* benefit if you went without all the little luxuries you have? Suppose you took out your central heating system and wore extra clothing instead? Suppose you sold your car and used the bus for all necessary journeys outside the village, but otherwise kept yourself within it? Suppose you restricted your meals to the very simplest but wholly nutritious essentials? I won't go on any more like this; I'm sure you've got my drift. Just imagine that you cut your standard of living down to the bare bones, and persuaded many others to follow your example? Would the money, food, petrol and whatever other commodities you saved, really help to provide food and shelter for the needy?

You do see, don't you, that if enough people withdrew from the clamour of the affluent society and began to live the simple life, those whose livelihood depends on the work which produces all the material goods you would have stopped buying, would become redundant. Not only would their families suffer, but there would be repercussions throughout the world of industry and commerce. Your own position in advertising, so dependent on the acquisitive nature of society, would at once be threatened. Once out of a job, you wouldn't be earning the money, some of which you are so concerned to save for the benefit of the poor.

What confusion and paradox! A new breed of poor would begin to arise, made unemployed by their own attempts to raise the other poor to *their* level! No, George, I do not mock your motives. They are good and right, and should not be cast lightly away. I am sure you realize only too well how past history rolls through the present day and into the future, turning the most fervent hopes into wild speculation. In this instance, it confirms again that wealth and poverty are illusions, the more so if you expect equality to be measured by them, and to see the results of your strivings towards it in your own time rather than mine.

Wealth and poverty are also relative. If a man has all he needs to protect and feed his family, is he not rich? Is it not because you have considerably more than you need that you regard the poor as poor? Do you ever wonder if the poor think of themselves as poor? They certainly think of themselves as cold, hungry, ill or lonely, but even rich men may experience those sensations.

If the so-called poor man has never mixed with anyone other than his own kind, he will not know poverty. It is only in comparing life-styles that you with plenty begin to use the words 'poverty' and 'wealth'. No more will a rich man, moving only amongst the rich, be aware of his riches. Before you invented the communications that brought remote parts of the world within sight and sound of one another, you did not know how 'poor' your brother in Africa or Asia was. Your conscience was untroubled. Should it be troubled now? After all, though you are aware of his plight, he is hardly standing on your doorstep. He is ten thousand miles away with a culture and philosophy all of his own that may well have no need of your charity.

Well then, George, should your conscience be troubled? Yes! Of course it should, but not because he is 'poor'. Why should you teach him the way of affluence when he will be better off without it? Give him affluence and you impart to him the greed of which, when you spare a minute to think about it, you are yourself ashamed. In part, your gifts to charity are only ointment for your conscience.

By all means attend to your brother's pain, homelessness, and hunger, wherever and whoever he is, but, for my sake, do not teach him that the way of the Western world is the way of truth and civilization, or that technological development is the god to be worshipped.

Teach him to plough and plant and produce better crops. Teach him the value of hygiene and antibiotics. These will give him the right kind of independence. Satisfaction in work and the health to enjoy leisure are the proper measures of freedom. Total financial independence will only tempt him to think, as you do, that he has the power to be self-sufficient.

Give him the opportunity to work and to feed his family; to lead a life which is full of creativity, fulfilment and

32

satisfaction; to run the race of life in such a way that death becomes a goal to be achieved, not a darkness to be feared. Is it not true, George, that you only fear death because of all the things in your present life from which it will separate you? You have accepted the gift of free-will gladly. You like to think you may do as you please, but you forget that in death I have a hold on you from which there is no escape. That this inevitable doorway through which you must pass into real life fails to put your present existence into its proper perspective, is due to your wilfully pushing all thoughts of it into the remotest corner of your mind.

Your 'poor' brother, who meets death daily, has a natural respect for it, unlike you desperate creatures of the Western world who, with the aid of multi-thousand pound intensive-care units and expensive drugs and surgery, would 'buy off' death if you could.

Do not think that I am belittling the compassion that you show to your fellows, but I will put to you a moral question. Is it right to spend vast sums of money to save one life, when that same money would provide enough food or medicine to prevent a hundred deaths elsewhere? There is a point in this paradoxical world of mine where compassion becomes extravagance.

Yet I have sown seeds of creativity within you so that you are capable of absorbing and emitting all kinds of powers and influences, receiving from and contributing to the people you meet. You remain incomplete unless you realize this. If you fail to realize it, you cut yourself off from the power that provides this growth because you cut yourself off from people. Creativity means being part of other people's riches and part of other people's poverty.

I see that you are still visiting Maudie in spite of your suspicions. Good. Don't worry about the possibility of coming into a small windfall because of your kindness. You expect Maudie to be humble enough to accept your help. There is little she can do for you. In fact one of the saddest things about Maudie is that she would love to have someone to show kindness to, but she has no one. You must find the humility to accept any financial reward she may have prescribed in her will. If one should be forthcoming when she's dead, and the heat of embarrassment scorches your bank statement, then you are always at liberty to pass Maudie's generosity on to someone else. A man's riches should encourage philanthropy, not guilt.

Being a complete person lies in rejoicing with those who rejoice and weeping with those who weep, using riches responsibly when they come your way, and being grateful for having enough, without feeling guilty because you have more than someone else.

Do you remember when you were first married? You had no television set. You take it so much for granted now the memory probably comes as a shock. You didn't have one because you couldn't afford one. You're only just old enough to remember that when television sets first went on sale it was only the wealthy few who could afford to own one. Yet, if the rich had not bought them to start with, the demand would not have increased so as to step up production and bring the price down. Now nearly everybody has one, at least a black and white set. Those who haven't yet bought a colour set are consoling themselves by saying they're waiting till the price of those comes down. And it *will*, or conversely, wages will have reached a level where the current price of a colour set becomes a bargain.

I'm having to use your language again, George. Earthly images. You must take care not to think that I'm suggesting you go out at once and buy a colour TV. I use this example simply to show how the possession of riches can sometimes assist in bringing what the poor man wants within his reach. You could apply this principle to men's needs rather than their wants, if only self interest didn't prevent it.

Which returns me to my eternal theme – growth. Self-interest prevents growth, for growth depends on giving and receiving. Guilt has no place in it, only sharing. Rich and poor alike have to contend with what history has wished upon them. Growth takes place in their meeting together and making decisions about each other as they share each other's experiences.

When the truth is known, at whatever hour I choose to reveal it, there will be no rich or poor. Those human terms describe only what you *think* you know, George. They attach only to your physical existence. You will not begin to know or serve me truly until you can think beyond that.

Rich and poor have freedom. Wealth is a burden, for the freedom it gives harbours greed and corruption, and needs to be protected by strong resistance to indulgence, and by responsible management. Poverty is a discipline whose freedom lies in limited responsibilities.

It is my love for you that gives you your freedom. Your love for me will determine how you use it. Covetousness destroys freedom all together.

Sorry to end on such a sombre note, George, but there it is. The choice is yours.

Yours sincerely,
God

P.S. Don't go on about your taxes. Pay them gladly. It's the one sure way in which you can contribute to other people's welfare.

... and a young man's fancy

Dear God,

What is it that makes me write to you? Is it anger, frustration, jealousy, disillusionment, or some virulent combination of the seven deadly sins? What is it, God, that compels me to get things out of my system by writing it down, all neat and tidy in a letter? I know it makes me feel as though I've written something important and searching when I see it here in black type, neatly double-spaced, but *you* know, I'm sure, that these letters are really a kind of safety valve when I'm feeling particularly bitter or confused about something. I suppose that's why you let me go on doing it; better to use *you* as a buffer for my aggression than the people who've actually provoked me, though I do sometimes wonder if I ought to make use of you in that way. Do you mind, God? I know *I* should be more than irritated if I was constantly being bombarded by other people's moans and groans. Don't you ever get fed up with us? I don't imagine that many people write you letters, but I bet there are plenty of prayers that make their way to you on wings of self-pity and resentment.

Well, anyway, here I am doing it again, in spite of myself. I just can't help it – or can I? I suppose I *could* stop writing here and now; go and read a book, watch the telly, or go for a walk. No! I couldn't settle to a book, there's nothing worth watching on telly, and it's too blooming cold to go out. Maybe it's boredom that drives me to writing. Maybe I'm just filling in time for want of something better to do, and flattering myself that you'll be interested enough in me to wade through several pages of drivel when it reaches you.

It's been snowing all day, that's what makes matters worse. Here I am freezing in a snow-covered, wind-ravaged Britain, while Edward Morris is sunbathing, I expect, in Ibiza – him and his delectable Joyce. I can just see them (can *you?*), idling on the beach, oozing with sun-oil.

Nice of them to send me a postcard, I suppose, but it only rubs salt into the wound. I don't know how they manage it, I really don't! It's the second time they've gone abroad for a holiday this year. Mediterranean cruise last time. They came back then all bronzed and virile. Well – Edward came back looking bronzed and virile. Joyce was more brown and mottled. Vigorous though, and relaxed. Did them good, I suppose.

It would do *me* good, too, don't you think? Can't you fix something? Sudden win on the pools, national lottery, *Readers' Digest* computerized raffle? No, I don't agree with such things. Anti-social, they are. What's the value of something I haven't worked for?

Good gracious! Have I just written that? A phrase about

'days of unprincipled youth' jumps to mind from somewhere. Perhaps you know who said it, God. Trouble with my youth was that it had too many principles. I eschewed lotteries because they relied on the principle of getting something for nothing at someone else's expense. I eschewed strong drink (isn't 'eschewed' a lovely word, God? In the Bible somewhere, I expect – Authorized Version, of course). I eschewed self-indulgence because I couldn't afford it. At least that was plain honesty rather than pretentious adolescent ideals.

What worries me now is whether my gradual, almost casual abandonment of these ideals (not deliberate, wholesale abandonment, you notice), is the result of having reached a plateau of maturity from which they acquire a different perspective, and become seen for the trivialities they really are when viewed against the greater evils of murder, rape, violence or whatever; or whether I've simply watered down my religion and morality, and gone soft to conform with popular opinion and social pressure, instead of standing alone.

I still can't afford self-indulgence, though. What does Edward Morris need *two* holidays abroad for? He could have stayed at home and done a spot of gardening or some jobs around the house. A change is as good as a rest.

Not much good to him though. He had his house professionally decorated from top to bottom just before he moved in. *And* there's no kids to smear jam on the door-handles, shoe-polish on the carpet, and acres of Lego-bricks and fluff under the beds. With both of them out at work all day, too, no wonder it always looks so spick and span.

When Rosemary and I were invited there to supper the other evening, we hardly knew whether to sit on the furniture or worship it. It was like walking into a page from a Habitat catalogue. Bit clinical though. Too clean and tidy. Not like a real home.

But how *does* he afford it, God. No, you needn't answer

that. I know. To begin with, he gets a far higher salary than I do. Of course, he *does* have a more senior position, but I don't doubt that being the managing director's son-in-law, he was well able to negotiate himself a salary well into five figures. Then there's Joyce out at work – market research interviewing or something. Never been very clear about what she did. That must bring in a good bit every month – and it's all theirs to do with as they please.

You know what *my* trouble is, don't you, God? I'm jealous. Luminous viridian, lime-juice, cabbage water, traffic-lights green, with envy. I don't deny it. We have all sinned and fallen short of the glory of God, and *I've* sinned, God, I know it. But I can't help it. The sin of envy is imposed upon us by the very injustices of life.

Why 'green with envy'? Something to do with the 'other man's grass', I suppose.

I mustn't be ungrateful. My grass has a *few* tufts of green here and there. Last week I paid just over ten pounds for a pair of shoes for Sara, and if she hadn't been a good kid and agreed to wear something plain and sensible instead of the highly fashionable, ankle-wrenching contraptions her friends are hobbling about in, I might have paid a good deal more. Rosemary always looks smart and attractive, in spite of the clothes in her wardrobe having hung there rather a long time. I can't blame her when she asks for more clothes. Whatever *I* say about her appearance she's bound to think she looks dowdy up against Joyce Morris in her swish Monica's Modern Boutique outfits.

She talks now about getting a job to boost the budget. I can't blame her; and it's all the fault of my youthful principles again. I've only just realized that prejudice works two ways. What I think are standards to be upheld are simply my own personal prejudices. Other people laughed at my foolishness when I said the family came first, and that's why Rosemary shouldn't go out to work when we were first married, and while the kids were growing up. They would need her. She would be their security. It was her duty as a mother to be there when they got home from school. Those who laughed at me, and gave their children their own front door keys, were the ones I thought were fools.

Now I'm not so sure, God. It's fifteen years since Rosemary last worked in a regular job. She's bound to be rusty. Changes have taken place in estate agents' offices. Procedure and qualifications have changed, so she's in no position to apply for the sort of job she had before we married. In any case, they seem to prefer young, dolly-bird types, flashing their long legs and tinted spectacles at would-be house purchasers, just to project the trendy, youthful image of a fast-moving, highly professional business.

Not much hope for Rosemary there. Maybe Woolworth's counter is about all she's fit for. No, that's unfair, but it's probably about as high as there's any point in aiming.

You haven't been at all fair, God. You burden us with principles, convince us that they are true, and then, when we stick to them loyally, you let us down. Social responsibility turns out to be a millstone, and yet, according to Jesus, his yoke is easy, and his burden is light. What kind of joke is that?

What with one thing and another, it's not easy to stop myself feeling hopelessly inferior. Failure seems to be staring me in the face. Edward Morris seems to have everything on his side – money, freedom, youth. *I'm* lumbered.

You know I'm not *old*, God, but forty is a dangerous age. You may have experience, but you haven't got the energy, or the arrogance to smile sweetly at people while you demolish their ideas with ruthless, whizz-kid efficiency.

I still can't think why you let me go to that interview at Jayson Media the other day. For that matter I can't think why they invited me when it was so evident they wanted a younger man. Why *did* you let me go? You *must* have known.

I know I only made the application in a fit of pique when Edward Morris was being so obnoxious about the Carlton-Seabury Biscuits account, but you needn't have let me sit there feeling more and more like a used dish-cloth as they fired their questions at me. I knew my stuff all right, though; but I suppose what they were looking for was some magic flair which they automatically assume lies with youth rather than age. They can't possibly know how much valuable experience, and how many useful contacts they've tossed away, not appointing me.

Of course! Why didn't I think of it before? A younger man would naturally command a lower salary. *That's* the reason! Or is it?

Writing to you, God, is like putting myself into a corner. Don't leave me there for too long. It's so terribly lonely.

Write soon,
George

P.S. Maudie felt a little better today. I helped her out of bed and she sat for a while at the window in the afternoon sun. It gave me as much pleasure as it did her. She even drank a cup of tea. Thanks.

Dear George,

Feeling lonely, are you? Well, what did you expect? Anyone who indulges in self-pity brings loneliness upon himself.

You think the sin of envy is about what other people have got. It isn't. It's about how little value you place upon what *you've* got. Worse – your failure to understand this causes you to belittle what others have or are. Having no confidence in yourself, you try to save face by discrediting those who seem to be succeeding in life. Edward Morris's home is as much home to him as yours is to you. Your attitude is inverted snobbery of the worst kind.

How often I've heard you moaning about politicians who conduct their election campaigns, not on the merits of their own party, but by attempting to discredit their opponents, pointing to all the faults they can find in their past record. Elected to power, they then go on blaming the previous government for all the problems they find themselves having to face. Envious of power when they hadn't got it, they discover how unwieldy it is when they have!

Do you not appreciate how lonely are the men and women who reach positions of power in government, or for that matter, the peak of promotion in any given field? It's not because they're short of friends, advisers or confidantes, but because important decisions rest upon their shoulders, and *only* theirs. Success or fame and glory are theirs if the decision proves to be the right one, but criticism and abuse if it's wrong. The higher you go, the more aware you become of the impossibility of making a decision which will please everyone. How do you think *I* feel?

Frequently the worst criticism comes from those least in a position to make a fair judgement. Is that what you're after, George, exchanging one kind of loneliness for another?

Envy promotes the desire to fill someone else's shoes because you think you could walk more uprightly, efficiently or comfortably in them. You want to discard the ones you're wearing because they pinch your corns. You feel inhibited. Believe me, if you change shoes, you'll only find the corns growing in different places. But enough of metaphors.

You are shrinking from your *own* responsibilities once you think you can shoulder the burdens of other men more lightly and capably. You even write to me as though I ought to make decisions for you that you'd rather not face yourself. Well, I don't mind being a safety valve for all the frustration you feel when decisions are hard to make and life seems to be all against you, but you'll not make real contact with me if you choose to travel life's road by the most undemanding route.

You've worked hard, George, and deservedly earned promotion, yet you're not satisfied. You do realize, don't you, that the ambition that spurs you on, makes you ungrateful as well as dissatisfied with where you've reached.

You write, too, about my burdening you with principles which you have gradually had to abandon as you've grown older and more experienced. Tell me, is it because you've matured, or because you've submitted your will to the god of ambition that you've let them go?

Maturity lies in the attempt to reconcile honesty with experience and faith. I agree that experience does make you more tolerant if you've been wise enough to learn from it. Only the childish cling irrationally to prejudice; it's often their only security. *Faith* must be your security. For the man who longs for the challenge of a new adventure, faith will lend more support than ambition. Ambitions are achieved or not, according to persistence or talent, or both, and then they are done with. Faith, once grasped, remains for ever, making failure and disappointment bearable. That's what Jesus meant by an 'easy yoke'. You have a saying too: 'A

burden shared is a burden halved', so I will remind you that I'm always pleased to hear from you.

Not that I blame you for wanting to prove yourself. Your lack of confidence disappoints me. It indicates a lack of faith. I'm quite aware that the application you made for that job at Jayson Media is one of several. You won't be at peace until you've explored all the likely alternatives to carrying on working under Edward Morris at Waverley Advertising. You just might jump out of the frying pan into the fire though, George. Had you thought of that?

But I won't discourage you. Go on applying. The only way to move hopefully forward into the ocean-like depths of the future is to dip an occasional toe into the surf. You'll be scanning the Creative and Media Appointments columns for quite a while yet, but don't get disheartened. Sooner or later you'll find a solution making itself clear. I haven't planned your future. Like everything else in my creation, it will evolve naturally, dependent as much upon your attitude to the world as upon the way of the world itself. The indecision and frustrations with which you find yourself wrestling at present will only benefit your character and help you to understand my will more perfectly, as long as you do not let them bring you to despair. Let me again recommend faith as a sure defence against pessimism and defeat.

There are two sides to envy – both with ugly faces. One is the way it encourages you to rate yourself as equally or more deserving of the glory that others appear to bathe in (with or without sun-oil)! The other is that it makes you regard yourself as of no account. But you matter to *me*, George. I insist that you remember that. How dare you feel lonely?

I have given you a home, friends and leisure. You have work that uses your creative talents and gives you satisfaction in the finished product (which is more than a good many can say, who spend their tedious days working on an assembly line, bored by repetition and never seeing the finished article); your wife and children love you and family life gives you a great deal of pleasure.

It is only because you take all these things so much for granted that they seem to be unexciting. I think a change of routine would do you both good. Why not let Rosemary go out to work now, if she can find something suitable? She naturally desires, as you do, the freedom that a different daily environment and the company of new people will seem to bring. You'll both benefit if she comes home with something different to talk about instead of greeting you with complaints about the chores of keeping house, and the irritation brought about by the clutter of Lego bricks and discarded screws and nails shooting up the Hoover nozzle.

The children are old enough now to value a little independence and to be responsible for themselves. The secret of bringing them up to be real people rather than pale imitations of yourselves, is not to be for ever 'on tap', but to be available when you're needed. They must begin now to recognize that you're entitled to lives of your own. By sticking to those 'principles' of yours when they were young, you've ensured that they know how much they matter to you, that you are reliable and consistent in your attitudes towards them. They know they can trust you because you have given yourselves to them. I know you will want to reply that you've done it rather inadequately. You haven't always been fair or kept your temper. You've worried because you haven't always given them as much of your time as Dr Spock would recommend. Well, no one's perfect, but your David and Sara are as aware of that as you are, and if you were perfect, what an awful burden they would have to bear. They'd never live up to expectations, would they? I hope you will take comfort and courage from those few remarks. They are the kind of experiences which encourage faith to grow.

Incidentally, those other 'principles', which you thought might possibly be prejudices in disguise, served as a healthy discipline when you were young. Now that you are older, and you choose to break some of them occasionally, they still act as a restraining influence. Don't envy the luxury of a 'high life' which is merely self-indulgence. You have health and strength of character which enable you to face life without the need to lose your identity or escape from reality in excessive drink or the excitement of gambling. Even now, I notice, you still feel a twinge of guilt when you buy a raffle ticket. Don't worry George, I shan't condemn you for that. Indeed, there are worse sins.

For instance; how dare you try to excuse your own faults by suggesting that the injustices of life make sin inevitable? You think life is unfair because you see some people, by their own efforts and my generosity, managing to achieve more than others. I suppose you think, because you go to church every Sunday, and proclaim what you believe to be the Gospel from the pulpit, that you're entitled to some

special consideration. You've no divine right to *anything!*
Unfairness is the illusion from which men suffer who think
life owes them something. Fairness is total impartiality,
George, and I will show you no more favours than anyone
else. I suggest you preach your next sermon on the parable
of the labourers in the vineyard!

But that's enough of that! You know, when you pause
for a moment's honest reflection, that you *do* have *something.*
It is nothing that can be measured in terms of worldly
wealth or success. Nor is it readily recognized by those who
do not know you well. You take too much to heart the
gossip and criticism which, in any case, you only *imagine*
goes on in Edward Morris's office or amongst the girls in
the post room.

I'm glad you still visit Maudie when you can. I alone know
your real worth. I know how conscious you are of failure.
It cuts most sharply those who try their hardest. They are

their own worst critics, *and* the most severe. Whatever happens, do not give up trying. That would be a sin.

Not that I am ever in haste to condemn anyone. That is, of course, part of the fairness of things. I say that because of your scepticism. But if everyone stands to benefit, what can be fairer? Besides, as you have discovered already, sin itself catches up with people eventually. Stricken consciences bring their own misery and loneliness. I am more anxious to fill the emptiness with love than to increase the misery.

That's where Rosemary, David and Sara have their part to play. Their reliance upon you is as much part of your security as theirs. The give and take which you have learned by living and sharing together is the essence of love. They through you, and you through them, make contact with me. My other name is Love.

As you hope your children will learn from experience, so too be ready to learn from them. Stay young with them by letting yourself go on growing. Do not, however, resent your increasing years. You seem, in your present mood, to be envying youth. Don't. Don't you remember the agonies you suffered in your youth? Would you go through them all again?

You fought bitterly with your parents over your first motor-bike. 'Only a moped', you said. 'Couldn't do more than thirty miles per hour', you said. You were lying too, when you denied that it would lead to bigger bikes as soon as you were old enough. You thought, more then than now, that you had envy under control, but you bought a 950 c.c. Norton as soon as you were seventeen.

You fought with them too, about Rosemary, remember? They said you had no sense to court a girl seven years older than you were. It would never work, they said.

You persisted all the same. And won! And it *did* work, didn't it George. But that wasn't envy, that was love. You know that, don't you? There must be a lesson in that somewhere.

Finally, when the rheumatics in your shoulder play up again, and you think you're old at forty, just try and see yourself through Maudie's eyes. Doesn't *she* envy *you*!

With good wishes and all my love,
God

. . . and a plain wrapper

Dear God,

You must have a passion for paradox. You've really set me a problem.

You saw how furtively I bought this glossy magazine at the newsagent's. You know where I keep it locked in the bottom drawer of my desk where young David's eyes won't see it.

No one's about at the moment though, so I can take a look. How am I supposed to react, God? On the front cover is a girl wearing nothing but shiny black gumboots, bending over with an open umbrella so that her breasts hang temptingly like ripe fruits as she thrusts her buttocks at me from the centre of the page, smooth and round, inviting caresses. Well – not caresses exactly. After all, it's only a photograph, but you have to admit, taken with such professional skill that you have to admire the clarity and composition no less than its subject matter . . . did I say *admire*? No, God, I don't mean that. I don't admire it one bit. No, that's not true. I think it's disgusting. Forgive me God, that's not true either.

If I turn the page there's another girl, rising from the sea, her wet open shirt clinging to her body, water dripping from her nipples, the wind in her wet, black hair giving her a wild and sensuous look which . . . God, help me! I almost burst into poetry looking at these creatures. What *am* I to do, God? I'm only human, and you *did* make woman to be attractive to me. If you'd made them all plug-ugly, I wouldn't have this trouble.

It's guilt that haunts me. Not because I bought the magazine, you understand. Well, you *know* that. You know I bought it purely for the purpose of research. I mean, how can I make Christian comment on something I've never looked at? But, God, the problem is I *don't* feel guilty when I look at these pictures, even though my upbringing taught me that such things were dirty and sordid. And *there's* the paradox! I ought to feel guilty, and I don't; so I do feel guilty because I'm not! Does that make sense? *I* know what I mean, anyway, and I expect you do too, so that's all that matters. But even when I try to convince myself that I bought the magazine for perfectly legitimate reasons, it's difficult not to suspect myself of dishonesty and self-deception. Hadn't I always wanted an excuse to buy one anyway? For how long have I simply lacked the courage, inhibited because there are people I know who would disapprove? I must say, the shop assistant was discretion itself, hiding the magazine beneath brown paper secured with Sellotape. I smuggled the 'hot goods' home in my briefcase, secreting them in the drawer to await a leisurely inspection after tea – a long-post-poned savouring of lascivious delights!

If only I were immune to temptation . . . but no; there was this girl once in a TV programme. Only a glimpse of her I had. One of those instant faces caught between two quick flicks of the vision-mixer's fingers; a face of creamy quality with long, dark lashes and glossy lips, immaculately made up. Young and innocent and vulnerable, she seemed to me, inviting warmth and tender caresses. I was *moved*. I can't deny it.

The commentary mentioned in passing that she was a stripper, but the camera had only shown her in long shot with many others, dressed all alike in white boiler suits and caps to match, dancing on stage at the Windmill Theatre. I'd seen no more of her than a fleeting glimpse of her pretty face, her slightly parted lips and bright eyes and, at her white throat, the large metal tag of the long zip that would open the front of her costume in one seductive movement of a slender arm.

More than all the naked bodies on the pages of the glossies, she tempted me. It was all in the mind, of course. I begin to think a man is more effectively seduced by his own imagination than by any exposure of female anatomy, however explicit.

I suppose I could keep the magazine locked away, God, never look at it again, burn it even. But I'd never be free of temptation would I?

Does desire diminish with age though? Certainly women lose their attraction for me as they get older, though I look in the mirror each morning and think *I'm* still quite handsome at 40. But, as I write, I'm remembering Maudie, so pale and withered. The doctor came yesterday while I was making her some soup. He wanted to examine her chest and asked her if she minded that I was there. She said she didn't, and with a curious logic, added that I'd been a comfort to her. I admired her for not minding, all the same, her being a spinster.

I wondered if anyone had caressed Maudie's body when she was young. No one wanted to now, surely? As she pulled back the neck of her nightdress for the doctor, I caught only a glimpse of greasy, yellowing skin. There was no arousal, no sensuality. There was neither embarrassment in looking, nor the desire to go on looking. If I felt any emotion at all, it was pity that poor Maudie, as far as I knew, had never enjoyed the pleasure of touching, and of being touched by loving hands, or the contentment of lying close and naked, next to another person whose body radiates with warmth, love and security. I went into the kitchen to attend to the soup.

If we were all born old, God, there'd be no such thing as lust.

I went down to the river this afternoon. Summer has come at last. There were girls along the river bank in sleeveless, low-necked dresses, and others in shorts or bikinis sunning themselves on the roofs of fibreglass cruisers. Janet, from the office, was there. There were men there too, I suppose. I didn't really notice. The staithe was a feast of slim legs and

glistening bodies; and how could they tell, as I sat on a wooden bench, eyes hidden behind dark glasses, whether I was looking at them or merely observing the ducks that paddled about in the scarce strips of water between the boats? Even if they could, how would they distinguish lust from admiration?

My face gave nothing away. There was only a stirring in my loins which fed my imagination, only to be suppressed by common sense and lack of opportunity.

How the imagination flatters! Which of those young attractive girls would have given me a second glance? Janet maybe. I do see her every day when she brings in the post; and if you believe all you see on TV, office secretaries are very popular as mistresses or casual girl-friends.

What vain speculation all this is, God. You know how happily married I am. You know the love and security there is in my family, and it isn't worth throwing away for the sake of a brief sexual encounter with a pretty young thing, fooling myself that a passionate but temporary affair will offer compensation as Rosemary gets older. *I'm* growing older too. Any compensation for diminishing powers will lie, I know, in the depths of the experiences we've shared together, the tears and struggles of nineteen years which have bound us together more closely with each year's passing.

I prize all this highly, God, so would there really be any harm in exercising my imagination with the aid of these sexy magazines? Would it be wrong to enjoy my fantasies? You know how unlikely it is that my dreams of secret assignations with beautiful sensuous women will ever become reality; and if my fantasies nourish my sexual prowess, well – so much the better for me and Rosemary!

I'm certainly not corrupted by nudes in full colour, pubic hair or not. When you've been married for nineteen years and shared the same bed and bathroom as a woman, how can a *photograph* corrupt? No woman in a glossy magazine is made any differently to Rosemary as far as I can tell. So there you are, God. You needn't worry about *me*.

There *are* a couple of things that bother me, though. I know there are worse magazines than the one I bought. When I say *worse*, I mean that they go a lot further than naked bodies, decorously or indecorously posed. I don't even know why I'm trying to explain when I expect you know exactly what I'm referring to – explicit sex, God, and rather more curious sexual activities, in plastic macs, with instruments of pain, or with animals.

Did something go wrong when you distributed the gift of sex – top quality sex for some, sub-standard sex for others? Or is there some gap in my understanding of human nature that resents activities which are abnormal to *me*? *Are* they so unnatural?

And who *are* the people to whom books containing photographs of these activities sell so readily at such high prices, and whose sexual appetites remain unfulfilled unless they indulge themselves vicariously in activities which the rest of us, who rate ourselves as normal, find distasteful and label as perversions?

Are they sick? *Are* they perverted? Or are they simply people so wicked that no compassion should be allowed to soften the condemnation they richly deserve, and which in time their indulgence will surely bring upon their own heads – if not upon some more sensitive part of their anatomy!

But how is it that those who must study pornographic magazines extremely closely in order to condemn them, are not themselves corrupted, when their chief complaint is of pornography's potential to corrupt others? Have *they* such mountainous reserves of spiritual strength and moral fibre that they can remain unsoiled, while lesser mortals are led astray into paths of self-abuse and degradation? God, you must forgive my impatience, or my naivety, but I can only translate their attitude as total arrogance.

Where is the sin in all this, God? Where does natural desire end and lust begin?

Shame on you, God. You've given us no guidance. Your own son was heard to say that every man who looks at a woman lustfully has committed adultery with her in his heart; yet, on another occasion when the scribes and pharisees brought to him a woman caught in the very act of adultery, he rebuked *them*, and merely cautioned *her*, saying, 'Neither do I condemn you. Go and sin no more.'

What a letter this has turned out to be. So *long*! I've given you more than a couple of things to think about, I'm afraid. It just shows how concerned and utterly confused I am about it all, but I'm sure you can untangle my ramblings sufficiently to work out an answer.

Write soon,
Yours sincerely,
George

Dear George,

I'm glad you've written to me at last about this question of sex and imagination. I've been meaning to raise it with you for some time, but you've never given me the opportunity. You needn't be ashamed of your confusion. Sooner honest doubt than strident voices raised in condemnation with no understanding or compassion.

The fact is I've built into you, and everyone else for that matter, the desire to find *me* at the heart of things. You get a glimpse now and again when you look for love in other people, and when you give love to others. A constant search is going on. You can't help it. Giving and receiving love is what makes the world grow, George. The trouble is, like everything else, love gets frustrated and goes off course. That doesn't mean there's something wrong with it. It simply has to retrieve its sense of direction.

What I wish people would remember is that sex is not a separate but an integral part of my creation – as natural and normal a feature of human existence as eating and drinking.

Incidentally, I've been meaning to ask you, George – What's wrong with you? Don't worry, I'm not suggesting you're abnormal. I wouldn't want you to think I'm comparing you with some of the sexual deviants (so-called) to which you referred in your letter. I think you should take a good look at yourself, though. Examine your own problems. How do they affect you? You've still got that rash on your arms and legs that suddenly appeared without any reason you could name. The doctor put it down to overwork and stress, do you remember? I happen to know, though you're naturally reluctant to admit it, that it appeared at the same time you had that prolonged difference of opinion with

Edward Morris over the Carlton-Seabury Biscuits project.

You see, there's no more wrong with someone who has a sexual deviation (and that, I'll remind you, is a human term), than with someone who's tired and miserable when things aren't going right, or someone who loses his temper, or another whose fit of depression takes him into a mental hospital for a period of treatment. *Your* frustration brings you out in a rash. Other people's frustration when their search for love and recognition ends in emptiness or rejection, finds expression through the sexual side of their nature.

The curious thing is that you've learned to accept, pity and forgive certain physical and emotional illnesses as inevitable and normal in the circumstances. Yet you single out sex for special treatment. Why George? How far is your disapproval evidence of fear? Do you find that sex is such a powerful physical force you can't reconcile it with spiritual energies?

How I wish you'd stop dividing human personality into convenient parcels. When I made you in my image, you were complete, body, mind and spirit, a harmonious unity. I long for the day, George, when this balance will be restored. You must keep trying.

And don't be put off by those platform moralists who would have you believe that life is amazingly simple, as they blithely label one thing right and another wrong. It makes them feel safe to think they've categorized human behaviour – as long as they're in the right category to start with, and never considering for a moment whether it may be fear or circumstance that put them there. A touch of 'There, but for the grace of God, go I', might lend them a little perspective. So might a little humility.

To condemn an individual is to point an accusing finger at society and therefore to point one at yourself.

By the way, I saw one of your advertisements the other day, George. Skilfully made it was. Your film editor certainly knows his job. Image after image in rapid succession; eyes, lips, tongue, teeth, flashing, smiling, laughing, biting, licking, inviting and seducing.

You've a good eye for a pretty girl too. You were delighted with the rushes, I remember. The final product was a really neat package, the best you've had a hand in, I'd say. Advertising needs compelling, irresistible images to lure the prospective customer. But then, you know that. That's why you permitted so much sex in that thirty seconds – and all for a bar of chocolate. So innocent, George, a bar of chocolate. No wonder you have to sell it as though it were a sin. Since the Garden of Eden I've known the attraction of forbidden fruit; but don't let paradox provide an excuse for hypocrisy.

I saw you at the river the other afternoon. You wouldn't find the girls half so interesting, you know, if the possibility of an illicit affair didn't excite you, however remote. Haven't you and Rosemary often said how much more fun your sex lives would be if you hadn't made it legal? Somehow, getting married has taken the spice and flavour out of it – like leaving that final teaspoonful of ginger out of the sweet and sour sauce. More paradox, George?

But don't be deceived. Imagination may offer a way of escape when familiar patterns threaten to become routine and humdrum, but sooner or later you'll have to return to the real world. You may find that fantasy has turned reality sour. Will you go on loving the fantasy and fail to give proper loving attention to Rosemary? What a pity if you find this world a let-down because it doesn't match the excitement of your dreams.

I don't know how you manage to confuse love with lust. The dividing line is clear enough. Lust is total self-gratification, taking all, giving nothing, thinking only of your own animal pleasure. The feeling is natural enough, but unrestrained, it belittles the value of a human being. Those who give in to lust demean their own personalities, and abuse those of their victims, however willing. Lust is always accompanied by lies or self-deception which undermine the security of personal relationships.

Love, as I'm sure you know, doesn't think about itself at all, being more concerned with giving all it can to the other person. The paradox is – there's that word again, George – that when it's given completely, love attracts love to itself.

Incidentally, you didn't have to make that rude remark about summer coming 'at last'. You run your business, I'll run mine. O.K.?

You asked about sin. If there *is* any, it springs from past traditions, nourished by fear, still lingering from the days when men thought of me as a God of wrath and vengeance, and tried to limit their lives so as to risk less punishment. In spite of the promise of abundant life that came with Jesus, they still prefer inhibitions to fulfilment. I'm not surprised. They think it's safer. And it *is*, but that's not the point. When Jesus rebuked the Pharisees in the incident you mention, it was because he knew their narrowness heaped up such guilt and resentment in their own souls, they simply had to find an outlet for it – and *did*, by picking on someone more vulnerable whose sins were less subtle and insidious than their own. Judgement of another makes such good ointment for your own soul – though it soothes but temporarily. How easily vice and virtue swap places. Dare I say the word again?

Paradox! There! It doesn't do to take a one-sided view of my world, George. What you call paradox, I prefer to see as the peak at which the two sides of a mountain meet. Without the slopes on either side, there would be no mountain at all. And how can you climb without a mountain?

For some, the pornographic magazine renders harmless the compressed lust which might otherwise explode into rape or sexual assault. For others it may precipitate those crimes. Natural functions must have natural outlets. The boy who demonstrates his love for a girl through sexual intercourse is only truly fulfilled if his partner responds with love. And I mean *love*, not passion. I have designed love as the most completely satisfying context in which the human body may express itself.

Deprived of love, what are people to do except seek second-rate substitutes, confusing the physical stimulation and the release of biological tension which masturbation or prostitutes provide, with the joy and satisfaction of giving and receiving love?

But I do not close my eyes to the potential for sin that lies in the inadequacy of human beings. When man's search for love is accidentally astray or deliberately misdirected, and some people choose to make money out of their confusion and rejection, then is the time for your moralists to step in; not to sit in judgement on the sexually disorientated, nor to ostracize them, nor to view them with the shallow pity that is condescension rather than compassion, but to take action against those who exploit their innocence and vulnerability.

They must dare to say that the purveyors of pornographic

material are labouring under an illusion. Their wares command high prices because it is *guilt* they wrap in glossy covers, but guilt and sex are not inseparable. And as soon as you remove the guilt, the attraction of forbidden fruit is gone, and with it the means of exploitation and the way to fat profits. The price would come down too, if there were no need to offset the probability of prosecution resulting in heavy fines.

Sold respectably and cheaply, as though sex were something one might reasonably expect to be depicted as happening between mutually agreeable adults, pornography might simply take its place amongst the information books, along with gardening, photography and model aircraft. You wouldn't call it pornography then, would you? The Plain Man's Guide to Sexual Activities, perhaps?

Am I going too far and too fast for you, George? I know that what I've just been saying would be hard for many to accept. It takes time to shed a burden of guilt and shame that has accumulated over many years. There wouldn't be a market for pornography if past generations had not designated certain areas of sexual activity abnormal. Who were *they* to judge? But now you have the sins of the fathers visiting you in your own time.

I think I've given you enough to think about for a while, George. Let me close on a personal note. Personal to you, that is. After all, you'll want to know what I advise you to do with that 'disreputable' magazine you bought.

Read it. Look at it. Not furtively, but openly. Feel no guilt or shame. Enjoy the beautiful bodies you see on its pages. It's no sin to admire a naked body. You've admired Rosemary's, haven't you? And hers owes nothing to Max Factor and clever studio lighting. Don't be lured into mistaking fantasy for reality. Give thanks for the pleasure you and Rosemary take in each other's bodies. That's real, and combined with the friendship, loyalty and trust that make your relationship more than a merely physical one, you will know a security and love that no picture in a magazine can either threaten or replace.

Yours sincerely,
God

P.S. I've just seen a student in Trafalgar Square, carrying a banner that reads 'Make Love Not War'. Seems like a fine sentiment to me, but I don't doubt some human will condemn it as being in bad taste, if not as an incitement to promiscuity. It has, of course, what you call *innuendo*. Beauty, you say, is in the eye of the beholder. In the mind too, possibly? Where, then, is filth and perversion?

... and a steak and kidney pie

Dear God,

Scented notepaper, I think, is rather common. Don't you? Or only for correspondence between the most sentimental of lovers. However, you may just detect, on receiving this letter, a faint but distinctive perfume.

Rosemary is out at a Church Council meeting. Sara departed yesterday on a week's camping expedition in Hampshire, and David is in Paris on a weekend visit with his school. Tomorrow and Monday, Rosemary and I will be alone together for the first time for years. You can bet we're looking forward to it.

For tonight, however, as you are no doubt aware, I am alone, and in addition to taking the opportunity to write a few lines to you, I am indulging in a pleasant little snack with a glass or two of home-made blackberry wine. Potent stuff, too! I shan't be surprised if it permeates the fibres of the notepaper. You must tell me if it has when you write back.

Rosemary's been having one of her baking days today, too. There's nothing to beat the combination of glowing red wine, good strong cheese and home-baked bread rolls. Cost? About twenty pence I suppose. A cheap and simple pleasure really, yet, in the comfort of a warm, quiet house, with Mike Oldfield's latest record playing softly on the stereo, it's sheer luxury.

Tomorrow the luxury will be rather more costly. I expect you know where Rosemary and I will be going. Chinese, of course! I think we shall sample a few of the more esoteric delights to be found on the menu, instead of accepting the set meal for two 'recommended by the management'. Barbecued spare ribs might be interesting, or we could try something really exotic. Fried squid perhaps, or bird's nest soup. Definitely there'll be one dish with sweet and sour sauce. My mouth is watering already at the prospect.

It'll be a very pricy evening out, of course, but it'll be worth it. It's not often enough that we have the chance to get away on our own. You know how it is, God. Most times when we eat out, it has to be midway through a weary shopping expedition on a wet Friday in the frantic city, the kids trailing and moaning behind us; all of us laden with bags and parcels that seem to take up half the restaurant. It has to be an economy businessman's lunch then. Four's a lot to feed and pay for.

Still, mustn't moan. Tomorrow night's the night! Even so, it won't match the meal I had the other day. Did you see *that*, God? You should have tasted it! Expense account dinner, of course. Note that God – *dinner*, not lunch. The sumptuous touch of class! Not the careful Waverley expense account meal either, but the full-blown reckless extravagance of Eastward Television. It was all to celebrate the completion of the series of programmes I've been involved in. We've called it 'The Persuaders'. You'll know that I wasn't too happy about that title. Sounds just a trifle sinister to me, a little slur on the motives of the people in the advertising industry. I did suggest a few others, but I was outvoted. In any case, I'm only paid to advise, so I don't suppose I'm expected to make creative decisions. I take the producer's point that a programme needs to have an overstated point of view or it just doesn't make good television. It's not that lies are told, exactly, just that certain aspects of the truth are emphasized. I expect we do just the same in the advertisements here at Waverley.

We shan't know how successful the series has been until we assess the ratings after transmission, but no one seemed worried by that. Acclaim was automatically assumed, and endorsed by several excellent courses and a choice of good wines. At least *we* were all satisfied that we'd made ten good programmes. No doubt you'll be taking me to task about that in one of your letters. Pride rearing it's ugly, sinful head again.

Never mind. I enjoyed the meal. Stayed sober too. I'm right to be proud about that, I trust. Anyway, I'd a long way to drive home afterwards. I didn't want to take any risks. I can't understand why so many people *do*. Bravado, I suppose. Demonstrating that they can hold their liquor while still retaining all their faculties. Why do you let them do it, God?

I'm glad to say I've never been drunk – well, I got a little tipsy once. Started with a couple of brown ales while working on one of the programmes. It reduces the tension, you know. Then we went to lunch, and I had a small dry sherry, and with the meal itself there were – oh, I don't know how many glasses of wine. My glass seemed to replenish itself. I was all right as long as I was sitting at the table. It was when I got out into the fresh air that my knees seemed somewhat loose at the joints as I tried to hurry across the road. It was only then I realized that I'd had more than was good for me.

Do you reach a point, God, where you're so drunk you don't know that you're drunk? Well – *you* wouldn't, or would you? Well, yes, you'd *know*, but I don't suppose you'd ever get that drunk. Being God, *can* you drink, anyway?

What *am* I trying to say? Have I had too much of this blackberry wine, already? I've only had one glass. Or is it two? Incoherent speech is one thing. Slurred writing is another! Let's have another go.

There must be a point where drinking for pleasure and relaxation topples over the edge of responsible behaviour into the abyss of self-indulgence and carelessness. Isn't that so? And it's bound to be sinful because it's likely to have repercussions that hurt other people. I've read about the awful cases of wife-battering and child-neglect that result from drunkenness, to say nothing of the terrible number of deaths due to drinking and driving. And people must *know* what the consequences are likely to be, God. Why *do* they do it?

It can't be inadequacy. Take Jim Robertson at the office. I like him a lot. He's intelligent and good at his job, but I'll never forget the embarrassment he was at last year's Christmas Party. Only you must know how much he had to drink. I suppose the temptation was inevitable when Waverley Advertising were footing the bill, and all the drinks were free, but I would have thought a normally level-headed bloke like Jim would have known when to stop. Why didn't he? He upset half the girls on the staff being over-merry and insistent with a sprig of mistletoe, and then ran his car into Sainsbury's front door on the way home. Spent two weeks in hospital.

Oh, God, I'm glad I have the sense to know when I've had enough. That sort of behaviour certainly adds weight to the views of the Total Abstinence Brigade. I can't say that I agree with them, though. I mean, would Jim have drunk less, or none at all, if I had provided him with a good example by limiting myself to fruit juice? I hardly need remind you that

Jesus was accused of being a glutton and a drunkard, yet clearly he saw his mixing with such people as a way of enjoying life, as well as an opportunity for offering salvation. I think the salvation he had to offer was something rather more than release from the evil chains of drink, too. I'd like your comments on that.

Do the total abstainers really think that by their example they will protect other men from becoming victims of their own weakness? I know how much I can drink, safely. Would I save another man by curtailing my own responsible drinking? I can't be certain, but it seems unlikely.

Drinking to excess is the real problem; don't you agree, God? In fact, I'd say that anything taken to excess is well on the way to sin. A rigid rule, like abstinence, only heaps up guilt. Take Maudie, for instance. I wrote to you about her quite some time ago. You haven't replied to that letter yet, though you've answered several others. I assume you received it.

Anyway, you'll know how guilty she felt about that glass of pale ale – probably the first she'd tasted in her eighty-four years. You wouldn't have wanted her to feel guilty about it, would you? If you're not careful, religion can turn all pleasure into a sin. There I go again. I don't mean if you, God, are not careful, I mean people in general. I don't seem to be quite myself tonight, God.

It's a bit of a poser, though, isn't it? I can well understand why some people would like a book of rules and regulations to help them steer a safe, moral course through life. It would certainly make things easier if you could tell us at exactly what point pleasures went too far. Would that be asking too much?

Maybe it is. I think I know what your reply would be – if we want rules we can always make them for ourselves. Self-discipline, that's the answer.

Goodness! At the rate I'm going, I shall have written your reply for you. Stimulated by this splendid blackberry wine, no doubt. You wouldn't deny us pleasure, would you? No, I'm sure you wouldn't. I have to confess to harbouring slightly guilty feelings about tomorrow, you see.

David came home from school once. He was eight or nine at the time, I think. You'll know the occasion I mean. He'd been made to feel guilty by one of the dinner ladies. 'I didn't want my dinner today,' he said, 'and Mrs Gittins said it was a wicked waste, and there were lots of little black boys and girls in Africa that'd be glad of a good dinner like that.' Did you laugh, God? I was tempted to, I admit, when he said he'd told Mrs Gittins that the black boys and girls could have it if they liked. I hope you noted that I also told him he was not to be so cheeky to Mrs Gittins, and it wasn't right to waste good food.

But I do wish I could feel that if I went without that Chinese meal tomorrow, it would do the world's starving poor some good. It won't, though, will it? So what's the point my feeling guilty?

Even if I ate so excessively as to rise from the table in a daze, capable only of staggering home to a couple of Alka Seltzers and a bed to collapse on to, any guilt would have to be attached to the harm I might possibly have done to my own digestive system, rather than the bread I had prevented from reaching someone else's mouth. God, what a muffle – nuddle – oh, rats! – muddle! I think the wine has got at the typewriter keys.

What *am* I writing about? Gluttony, I think. Most sins, I reckon, hurt other people. That's the only criterion that makes them real sins. Maybe gluttony is one of those little sins that hurt only the sinner and nobody else. Is that right, God?

Have you or have you not given us our bodies to do as we like with? Where's the abundant life that Jesus talked about if we have to be tethered by strict discipline and narrow moral laws, hardly daring to enjoy ourselves lest we open temptation's doors to the hopelessly inadequate who would probably yield to temptation whether we had anything to do with them or not. The poor ye have always with you!

Besides, if there is life after death, does it really much matter whether what we do to our bodies causes us to die soon or late? The consequences of over-eating, drunkenness, or any other abuse – sexual promiscuity, smoking, or drugs, for instance – are surely no greater risk than that of stepping under a bus while out shopping.

What's more, you know how advanced food research is these days. There seems to be nothing we can eat in which the scientists have not discovered some fattening, cholesterol developing, mildly poisonous, slowly addictive, or otherwise harmful ingredient. We seem to have an equal choice between starving to death quickly, or eating ourselves to death more slowly!

> To all that's low in carbohydrates, Alleluia!
> To all that's high in polyunsaturates, Alleluia!
> For ever and ever, Amen!

Must close now. I can hear Rosemary's key in the lock.
Looking forward to your reply,
Yours sincerely,
George

P.S. The cheese is excellent too. Danish Blue – sounds like a pornographic film, doesn't it? – I wish I could send you some, but I fear it would spoil in the post.

Dear George,

If you had only kept a copy of your last letter, you could read it now and see for yourself the silly, childish, humour that you are prone to after only three glasses of blackberry wine. The odour was not apparent on the notepaper; the influence most certainly was! You see how easily you deceive yourself. You think you're capable of holding more liquor than you actually are. It's a wonder that your letter made any sense at all.

You were of course wise to relax. You've been working extremely hard lately with your additional commitments in television. I'm particularly glad that you found time to write to me. Busy-ness is so often an excuse for neglecting things that really matter.

However, you could have relaxed quite adequately with one glass of wine, and I would not have objected to that; but two was foolish, and three was sheer arrogance. You knew it would loosen your knee joints and make your head spin. That's why you stayed sitting down, not even getting up to turn the record over. And when Rosemary arrived home, you let *her* make the coffee. Any decent fellow would have made it for her when she'd walked home through the cold, dark village streets from a none-too-happy Church Council meeting. Still – if you'd got up before you'd had the coffee, you'd probably have fallen over. Then she'd have had to cope with you concussed on the carpet from banging your head on the typewriter, or something equally ridiculous. Either way she couldn't win. Now, perhaps, you see how selfish it was. And there you were, thinking that because you were alone it wouldn't matter. You thought you'd harm no one. Well, there may have been no physical violence committed, but it was extremely inconsiderate of you. There are such things as sins of omission, you know.

Never mind. You are forgiven. At least you are still keeping in touch with me, and the questions you raise in your letter indicate your honest intent to meet my requirements as far as is humanly possible – always supposing you know what my requirements are!

I know that you think I am especially unhelpful on moral questions. My answer, as you well know by now, is always – Love. Unfortunately you find it difficult to apply. I know it is a general rather than a particular rule, but I prefer to leave you with options open, so that the responsibility of decision-making assists your personal growth. Do you think I want to be served by a regiment of zombies? I would sooner have you fail than be bored by the repetition of success engineered through you by the imposition of my will on yours.

What worries me, though, is when you choose to suspend the use of your own mind, and here, I hasten to add, I am not only talking about the self-indulgence of over-eating or drunkenness which so stupefies the mind that it is no longer in control. I am concerned about personal relationships and attitudes to others which are so thoughtless and selfish that they encourage the insidious growth of sin in almost everyone.

Do you remember Alan Griffiths? Well, you will now, even if you had forgotten. He was that skinny little six-year-old who lived next door to you before you left Northampton. Skinny! He was ten when you finally moved house, and by then even you had noticed how fat he was getting. If you had seen the huge school dinners he tucked away, the enormous second helpings, you would hardly have wondered why he was growing so large. But you ought to have suspected that the reason he ate so much had less to do with his appetite than with the interminable rantings his over-anxious mother poured on his head. You moved house to come to your job with Waverley Advertising, but I know you'll recall how glad you were to get away from those high-pitched tirades.

It was enough, you said, to peel the paper off the walls!

Poor Alan! He wasn't very bright, but his mother did so want him to be successful. His school reports gave little academic promise, and he took them home in fear and trembling. She never struck him. She just got herself wound up and screamed away at him like a saw-mill until she'd reduced him to a blubbering, crumpled heap. If she *had* struck him, it would at least have been the beginnings of human contact. She never cuddled him once, not properly anyway, only in a stiff embarrassed way. She'd wanted a girl when Alan was born.

When one human being is rejected by another, he has to find compensation somewhere. Alan found it in food. You should see him now. He's twenty-two, ungainly and obese. He can't walk far without losing breath and needing to sit down. His doctor can only advise him to diet, but that of course needs confidence and willpower. His mother has eroded most of that.

What I hope you are learning from this sad case, George, is that some people's 'sins' – note the inverted commas – are wished upon them by the thoughtlessness of others. Gluttony may have been Alan's 'sin', but the devil was his mother.

However, food and drink are not only essential for survival. As you have already discovered, they can be a pleasure in themselves. They contribute effectively to the warmth and relaxed atmosphere around the family table. I wish, in fact, that a few more families would find the time to have a meal together. It is the only real fellowship. It is an opportunity for communion which is too often denied by the preference for TV snacks and by meals at odd hours for solitary members of the family arriving home from school or work. Eating alone is sad.

But I digress. I am concerned for those whose sin is drunkenness or gluttony, especially when they are victims of external pressures which they find themselves too feeble to resist. The real sin is not that they drink to excess, but that they are convinced that to do so is to prove their manhood. Regrettably the company they keep encourages the notion that drunkenness equals the achievement of status. Are they really *friends* who insist on frequently topping up another's glass?

You ought to know exactly what I mean. Your own experience is a case in point. After that short but potent catalogue of drinks you had at Eastward's expense, you were fortunate to get across Prince Edward Street all in one piece. At least you became aware, as you lurched towards the opposite pavement, narrowly escaping the wheels of a bus, that you had consumed more than was good for you. The fact that you fell victim to another man's folly does not excuse *you* all the same. You could have resisted. If your glass had simply remained full, he could not have gone on topping it up. Some moral choices are easy to make. You should have made that one.

Others, I admit, are less clear. Even so, many 'sinners' – note the retention of the inverted commas, George – are victims of society rather than offenders against it, and are frequently condemned by greater sinners than themselves.

You mentioned in your letter about the description of Jesus as a glutton and a winebibber. This picture of him, you realize, is hardly Matthew's, and certainly not Jesus' own. Look it up in the gospels George and read it there for yourself. Jesus himself used the words as descriptive of what some people were saying about him, and he made it evident that in judging him they were exposing their own attitudes to judgement. Many of his critics, the Pharisees amongst them, were blind to their own hypocrisy. In condemning the gluttons and winebibbers, they were conveniently distracted from the poverty and loneliness which had driven the 'sinners' to seek satisfaction in physical pleasures. Their own sad poverty lay in the inadequacy of their personal resources with which they might have nourished the souls of the friendless and needy.

You're quite right to think that Jesus offered rather more

than release from the lure of liquor. He offered a sense of direction in life that made it unnecessary for men and women to run away from life, obliterating misery and depression with an alcoholic haze. The faith in me that he pointed to, breeds self-confidence and determination, drives away fear and removes guilt by promising forgiveness. What is there to run away from when you have faith in me? Life is not too much. Quite the opposite; life is not enough! Faith looks for challenge, not escape.

That is why you must find the point of balance between the self-indulgence of gluttony and the challenge of meeting the needs of other people. Relaxing with good food is pleasant, and not sinful – a little of what you fancy does you good. Enjoying good food, well-prepared and attractively served is a ceremony of thanksgiving. I am glad when I see you relishing the fruits of the earth which I have given you. Many are the times when meals have brought friends and families together. I have enjoyed being at a good many birthday teas and wedding receptions, not only to see people enjoying good food, but enjoying each other's company too. However, I do regret the notion that prevails in some quarters that a good time can only be measured by the number of empty bottles. The foolish man's 'good time' is spent in such oblivion – and with such dire results the morning after – what would he know about his 'good time'? For his friends, his 'good time' may have been their embarrassment.

From the effects he feels the following morning, he ought also to realize the harm he is doing to his body. Alcohol is a poison, you know; it dulls the brain and rots the liver. You raise an interesting question when you ask, since your bodies are yours, can you not do as you like with them? Of course you can – as long as you're not expecting me to intervene when your body suffers the natural consequences of abuse, and as long as you're prepared to accept the pangs of remorse and regret that accompany the harm or grief those consequences may inflict on other people.

Herein lies a natural link with your questions concerning life after death. Life beyond death is simply the putting of this life into its eternal perspective, enabling you to grieve or rejoice over the actions for which you are responsible, including those shameful actions which, even more shamefully, you sought to lay at someone else's door. It is the way to maturity too, if you can come through the experience with your faith still intact; but to greet death too early as a result of carelessness leaves many years of human existence unused and wasted. And I *mean* 'carelessness'. Early deaths through suicide are a different matter. Death which results from self-indulgence is not a deliberate choice as suicide is; it is the outcome of complacency, a sin which is a close neighbour of another of the seven deadlies, sloth.

Of *course* it matters whether you abuse your body or take good care of it. It is a gift. It has potential that I long to see fulfilled.

For this reason – though it may surprise you – I am less concerned with the consequences your greed may have for others than with the effect it has on you personally. Real, consuming greed retards your growth, reducing you to the level of the wild beasts from which you have evolved, and whose natural savage instincts I had hoped you were leaving behind you. Would you return to the jungle, George, where the law of survival is the only law? Is it still to be every man for himself?

Total self-indulgence of any kind dulls sensitivity to the needs of others. If you allow yourself to be dehumanized for the sake of so-called pleasure, what hope is there for the rest of humanity?

But all is not lost. Your letter tells me that. You are clearly anxious that your brothers in the underdeveloped parts of the world should be fed. Good. You can support one or more of the many voluntary organizations which exist for that purpose. You can write to your M.P. and persuade him of the urgency with which foreign aid needs to be increased,

especially for that area you call the Third World. You can remind him of the great piles of surplus food which stand rotting every so often on European farms or in dockside warehouses. There is really no reason which satisfies me why this food should not be shared with those who are starving. You have the transport and the communications. Only the lack of a profit motive undermines the will to see that it is done.

One of the troubles also is that too many of you think that you stand alone, and that your single voice is inadequate and certain to go unheeded. Take courage, George. Make your protest. Your example may be sufficient to lend courage to others. You risk, of course, the danger of being labelled a vociferous minority, but so were Christ's apostles.

All the same, take care. People are proud. They do not take readily to charity. Poverty does not automatically breed humility. Besides they would much prefer to grow their own food and satisfy the needs of their people by the labours of their own hands than become for ever dependent on handouts from rich relations. Tractors and tools and seed are better gifts than food parcels. While Common Market representatives are discussing the embarrassing mountains of surplus butter or beef over their expense account lunches, crops could be springing up in the soils of Africa and Asia. Even I make you work for your living. It gives you self respect and nourishes faith. There is a point at which what you regard as generosity would feed a man's body but destroy his spirit. I am always concerned that man should reflect me in his wholeness.

Still worse – with your gifts of refined foods from Western civilization you may even contribute to the destruction of his body, swapping his starvation diet for one that breeds cirrhosis of the liver and diseases of the heart.

I can appreciate your feelings of remoteness and inadequacy, but in my time, not yours, all will be well. It does you credit to look for short-term solutions, but never lose sight of the more distant horizon, beyond which all that causes you so much concern now will be seen in perspective.

You can, however, be assured that there is value in more local and immediate gestures. I noted with satisfaction that the steak and kidney pie which Rosemary cooked for lunch on Sunday was big enough to leave a tempting portion for Maudie. I know she only managed a spoonful or two of the gravy. Rosemary's rich pastry and the meat were too much for her, but she really did appreciate the kind thought. There is much to be said for the advice of the man you call Saint Paul. You've read his letter to the Christians in Galatia – 'Let us then do good to all men as opportunity offers'. He goes on to say, 'especially to those who belong to the Christian household', a limitation I would personally object to; but never mind, his heart was in the right place, so let it be.

When the opportunity doesn't present itself to you there's

not a lot you can do, so there's no purpose served by worrying about it. On the other hand, if something worries you enough then you'll just have to *make* the opportunity, won't you, George? It certainly won't make itself.

   With love,
   God

... and a matter of application

Dear God,

You're lucky to get this letter at all, you know that, don't you? Haven't you ever had one of those black days – when you were making the world, perhaps – when you just didn't want to be bothered any more; lost interest in the whole project? No, I don't suppose you did, though I wouldn't blame you if you'd lost interest since, the way things are.

Anyway, I'm having one of those black days today, though you'll know it's only one in a whole black fortnight. Maybe the fact that I'm writing to you is a sign that I'm emerging at last from the tunnel of gloom and despondency.

I don't know what's the matter with me, honest I don't. Perhaps you'll be good enough to write and tell me. I feel so lethargic, and I can't think of a single reason. I know I've been working rather hard lately, but I'm sure it's not over-tiredness that's affecting me, it's more like can't-be-bothered-ness.

I don't feel like doing *anything*. The garden needs digging. If I don't go out and attend to it soon, before the growing season starts in earnest, it'll be knee-high in weeds, and then it'll be twice the job it is now. But, I just can't be bothered.

I did muster enough energy to go to the library and borrow half a dozen thrillers, but none of them seem to take my fancy now that I've got them home; so I switch on the telly, just to see what's on – the sort of absent-minded button pushing that I'm always telling David not to do. 'Either watch something properly, or switch it off' – and any old rubbish passes the time. Even the occasional gem of a pro-gramme that sparkles through the fog of bland situation comedies or glossy American car-chasing, gun-toting, crime-detection trivia, does nothing to stimulate or entertain me. I get so *bored*, God.

Do you know what boredom is? Have *you* ever been bored? I wonder sometimes if you can really appreciate how I feel when you've never been through the experiences I've undergone.

Can you do anything for me, God? Perhaps I should go to the doctor and have a thorough check-up, but he told me the last time I went to him feeling like a night-starvation case for a Horlicks advertisement, that they didn't believe in tonics any more. I'm sure it's what I need. It's a funny thing to say, but I think I'd be quite relieved if he found that there was something seriously wrong with me. At least there'd be an explanation for this physical go-slow.

It's not that I'm lazy. I sit at home frustrated by my inertia, consumed with guilt as I think about all the things I'm leaving undone. I know that if I made up my mind to set about all the outstanding jobs I'd finish with the most marvellous sense of achievement. But I just don't make a start. It's easier to sit and feel guilty than to get up and actually do something. Yet it's so confusing to care and not care at the same time. Is it willpower that I lack? What's happening to my mind?

Maybe it's reaction after all the hard slog I've done for Eastward TV. I *did* feel under pressure when they gave me those deadlines to meet. I met them though. *That* was satisfying. I hated the pressure at the time but I feel lost without it now. Maybe I just haven't given myself long enough to wind down.

What a curious thing intelligence is, God. I sometimes think you gave it to us to confuse rather than enlighten us. What I mean is – I can convince myself either way on this problem if I think about it long enough. I can sit with my feet up, telling myself that it's a just reward for a period of hard work, that I deserve some time to myself for recreation and relaxation, and I needn't feel at all guilty about it; I need to recharge my batteries. Or I can admonish myself for sitting about doing nothing, telling myself that relaxation is only another word for idleness; an excuse. Then I go completely perverse, and blame it all on the mind-boggling confusion this intellectual see-saw produces. If I weren't so bewildered by the effort of coming to terms with it, I would be able to work or relax as I choose.

God, you've made a mess of me. You're as bad as the politicians. We're going through the farce of a General Election at the moment, as you know. The more the candidates talk, the less convinced I am that I want to vote for any of them. I know it's all promises anyhow. Once either party gets into power they're bound to discover that their glib solutions, aired on public platforms, hardly match the realities of government. Why can't they be honest enough to admit it? I hope that doesn't sound too cynical or too disillusioned, God. I know they're only people – human beings like me. I'd probably sound and act a lot worse in their positions; but when there's nothing positive to vote on, what am I to do. Where would *you* put your cross on the ballot paper? It's all right for you – God the Impartial. You remain aloof from the hurly-burly of the hustings, abstaining without fear of criticism. But people tell me it's my right and privilege to vote, and to neglect to do so would be to snub democracy. Others say that to abstain from voting is a perfectly valid and positive action, a way of protesting against the futility of the system, or the inadequacy of the candidates.

There, I've done it again. Blast intelligence! I've argued both ways and I can't discern any greater merit in one argument than the other. If I don't vote I'll be accused of apathy or complacency; if I do, I'll feel I'm only making a stab in the dark.

Which reminds me – Maudie tells me she has a postal vote. I drove out to see her last Sunday afternoon at the little Cottage Hospital at Merrill Heath. She's been there a fortnight now. I dare say this will be the last election she'll cast a vote in. She talks quite openly about dying, now. I suppose it was moving to the hospital that finally confirmed the seriousness of her illness. She hasn't lost her sense of humour though. 'Like a lot of elephants, we are,' she said to me, nodding at the other patients sitting around the common room, 'it's where we all come to die.'

'You're no elephant,' I said, 'you're as thin as a rake. Do you get enough to eat in here?'

'I get what I need,' she said. 'They *do* look after us in here. It's nice to be looked after when you've come to the end of the road.'

She was quite matter of fact about it, but not morbid, and certainly not afraid. She seemed ready to welcome the release from pain and frailty that death would bring. Her resignation was not resentful or despairing; in fact, the hospital, for all that it was locally well known as the place where terminal cases came to spend their last days, was a place of hope, aided no doubt by the quietness of the atmosphere and the warmth and patience of the staff. Despite the fact that Maudie had always kept herself to herself, and was not much liked by the villagers, I get the feeling that she had never regarded herself as being completely alone. *You* were the secret she kept hidden in her heart all her long years. Now that she is near the end of her human existence, she seems, at last, to be letting a little of what you are show through.

How did I come to be writing about Maudie? You see what a state I'm in, God. That's mental laziness. I can't even keep my mind on the subject I set out to write to you about. I do it in church sometimes; have you noticed? During the prayers, instead of concentrating on what the preacher is saying, I start pursuing some thought of my own. When I return to the preacher's words, I don't know what he's talking about because I've lost the thread. A little self-discipline is what I need, I expect. It all boils down to a question of being able to make decisions. If I'm honest, I've got so many things to do, I can't make up my mind which to tackle first. Often the simplest solution seems to be leaving them all alone until one of them absolutely cries out to be done soonest. Given time, priorities make their own way to the top of the list.

Good in theory, madness in practice. As likely as not I'll find two or three have arrived at the top of the list at once. Then I haven't enough time to give them all the attention they need. Procrastination breeds inefficiency. Even a small amount of early preparation helps. Perhaps I take on too much in the first place. Crowded hours and wasted days! It's not that I'm lazy, really. It's just that I'm such a bad organizer. But what's life *for* if it all has to be planned in fine detail like a school timetable? 'What is this life, if full of care, we have no time to stand and stare. . . ?'

We should go mad if we couldn't escape from the turmoil of this busy world you've put us in. 'Be still, and know that I am God.' Isn't that the motto? Or am I being lazy again? Using someone else's words saves me thinking of my own. Maybe I can quote something else shortly!

There seems to be a lot of words about lately. Every national or world crisis seems to sprout a commission which subsequently sits for months or years before giving birth to a report of many thousands of words and making recommendations which, once neatly bound and sold by Her Majesty's Stationery Office at £5.95 a copy, is distributed to the offices of important people, summarized by pundits in the press and discussed to pieces on TV, and finally consigned to shelves where gathering dust slowly buries it. Sound and fury, signifying nothing? There, I said I'd come up with another quote. So much for words, words, words! Actions speak louder! There, that's another.

It is as though by discussing our problems and reducing them to carefully worded prose we believed we had solved them, or at least done the most that could be expected, lubricating our consciences with the oils of verbosity.

But God, I ask you, is there any alternative? I'm just as bad. Confession time again! I gladly make donations to Oxfam, Christian Aid, Amnesty International – you name it, I'll give to it. *That's* easy, but I don't *do* anything.

I suppose I'm what people refer to as a 'moderate'. Others might call it 'sitting on the fence', but I rarely come across an issue where the arguments are clear-cut, and a solution possible without compromise. It seems to me that compromise is a modified form of sacrifice – which, I'm sure, you would commend. I don't believe in hasty decisions, especially when I can see merit on both sides, and more especially when I don't know enough about an issue to be able to make an informed judgement. I *do* get irritated when people at the office bristle with indignation at the apparent indecision of the Prime Minister or the Home Secretary in some matter of industrial unrest or crime. They've usually half-read – or half-heard over a TV snack – a sensationalized statement of half-truths, and after throwing in a few ill-thought out prejudices of their own, declare themselves competent to pronounce upon the issue. There's sloth for you. Mental torpor.

'Wait and see,' is often my reply; leave it to those who know the details of the case and the people involved. But there's no restraining them once they get steam up. 'Wait and see', they say, 'and it may be too late, and anyway, what do *they* know?'

'They' – the derisory all-embracing pronoun for anonymous authority. I want to say to them, 'Well, what do *you* know?', but there isn't any point, really. They see my open mind as a gap through which any injustice can roll on greased wheels. Maybe they're right. They *do* seem very positive. What am I?

Maybe I *will* go and see the doctor, if only to suggest to him that my head needs examining.

> Yours sincerely,
> George

Dear George,

Let me come straight to the point. Laziness is not facing facts, and that's just what you've avoided doing in your last letter. I know that constantly at the back of your mind are nagging worries about your future. Unlike Maudie, whose future is certain and not without hope, yours seems bleak. You have carefully avoided mentioning the continuing dissatisfaction you're finding at Waverley, and the further unsuccessful applications you've made for other jobs. Dishonesty and self-deception are laziness too, and you're guilty of both. Your lethargy is only an outward sign of the sick condition of your spirit. Maudie is in better condition. Your heart is not in your job at Waverley any more; I've known that for a long time. It's a period in life that many men go through. Their youth has gone and the first signs of old age are beginning to be felt. Energy and motivation are waning with a consequent decline in self-confidence; though it doesn't have to be an inevitable decline.

But you cannot separate body from soul, and the poor health of your mind and spirit is producing physical symptoms. It would be a good idea to consult your doctor. There's nothing seriously wrong, but there will be if you continue to think you can cope under all the worry and pressure that life is currently thrusting at you. Your rash has broken out again, your sinuses frequently throb and blur your vision, and you've begun to get those headaches quite regularly now. Go on, admit it. If you don't you'll live to regret it.

The truth is you're trying to escape from something that you've come to regard as a burden, but you've cluttered your way of escape with all manner of conditions, so you musn't be surprised if you can't get out. You don't want to move house if you can help it; you don't want to upset David or Sara's schooling; you don't want to take a cut in salary; and you are looking for a job that will use your experience and know-how in advertising, because it's the only thing you really know anything about. Let me say plainly to you that you'll only achieve the change you're so anxious to make if you alter those conditions.

Personally, I would sooner see you make your way successfully *through* your present crisis than offer you a way around it or away from it. Defeatism is sloth too.

But don't jump to any hasty conclusions. You'll begin to think that I'm advising you to stay with Waverley, so as to remove the uncertainty by ignoring the Creative and Media Appointments columns, and that the way through that I urge you to follow will not involve any change of direction; but no – the way through will require you to consider all manner of possibilities. You mustn't expect the way to be easy, but as long as you have an application in the pipeline you will at least have that glimmer of hope to keep you from total despair.

You can't have it both ways, you know, George. You want to change, but you want to play safe. You're in a rut. Only by taking risks with your future will you discover the challenge and obtain the stimulation that your life is lacking at the moment. Ruts – that is to say, the routine which continues to make you bored, must be tackled routinely. Why not make a list of the jobs you feel so guilty about leaving undone? And not just a single heading for each one. Break each individual task into separate parts, and mix them all up together for a bit of variety. The mental exercise of this will do you good for a start.

Take the gardening, for instance. Something like this: Dig two rows; mow lawn; dig two more rows; gather up the mowings; dig two more rows; gather up garden rubbish into a bonfire; gaze thoughtfully for ten minutes into the flames; dig two more rows; have a cup of coffee; dig two more rows . . . and so on.

Does that sound too ridiculous? I can assure you, you'll find it a curiously relaxing way of going about the chores, especially if the weather's fine for you. The satisfaction you'll get from having all those irritating little jobs behind you will be tremendous. Routine doesn't have to be dull. Application with imagination, that's the motto.

In your present mood, you were coming dangerously close to relying too much on the power of faith. I know it's said to move mountains, but it doesn't dig gardens all by itself. I know too that in previous letters I have commended faith as a way of putting your problems in perspective, but it won't solve them for you on its own. 'Faith without works is a lifeless thing'; and knowing your Bible as well as you do, I'm sure you'll know where that quotation comes from. It's no good just waiting around, hoping for a miracle to happen, when you're capable of accomplishing so many things by your own efforts. It would be as though in using those quotations in your last letter you were expecting other people's words to work like some magical incantation to conjure away your problems in a puff of smoke. There's no harm in borrowing other people's words, quoting from the Bible or Shakespeare or wherever you care to find your inspiration or guidance. The fruits of other people's experience has much to teach you, but you must never allow it to become a substitute for your very own personal experience, and always provided you are alert enough not to confuse eloquence with truth.

I find myself worrying from time to time about those students of the Bible whose spiritual growth has come to a halt at the point where the Bible leaves off. It is as though I'd had nothing to say to the world since its last words were written. I sometimes feel so constricted; stitched and bound, you might say, in soft black leather with gilded edges.

It's as though you were still voting M.P.s into your House of Commons to protest about child labour in the coal mines. Those days are over and done with. Surely the least I can expect is that my people will put their minds to discovering what I'm up to in their twentieth century.

Which brings me quite conveniently to that question you raised concerning the imminent General Election. Of course you must cast your vote. Democracy is about as near as you'll ever get to that fairness which is impartiality. Lacking omniscience, what more would you hope to achieve? Whoever finally represents your constituency will do his best. When all's said and done, whatever party flag he rallies under, he *is* an individual. I know you would want to place a question mark over that statement, but have you ever considered that to lack faith in your fellow human beings is to lack faith in me? Their potential is my potential.

You have an unfortunate tendency to pray 'Deliver us from evil', when you've no clear idea what the evil is. You simply categorize it as one, because you fear what you do is not immediately understand. You rely too readily on instinct and first impressions; although to be fair, you did give Maudie the benefit of the doubt, when you moved into the village and found it hard to find anyone with a good word to say for her. Too many people rely on second-hand opinions. That's sloth for you. They really ought to find out for themselves.

To come to another matter. I'll have no more of your disparaging remarks about the gift of intelligence. If yours is so perceptive that it readily sees both sides of an argument and persuades you to exercise restraint before making a judgement, then you should be rejoicing, not complaining. I know it makes decisions difficult, but it does ensure that when you finally make one, it is more likely to be acceptable to both sides than if it were made in haste. You must not allow expediency or impatience to rule the day.

Just look what happened when David and Sara were quarrelling the other day; that pointless argument over a TV programme. David wanted to watch that comedy show that Sara thinks is too silly for words, and David, being in one of his 'moods' only wanted to watch in order to annoy her, anyway. So you simply switched the set off; a quick, decisive action – which you regretted for the rest of the evening! David's mood got blacker, and Sara retired, hurt and miserable, to her room because, although her natural reticence prevented her from saying so, she'd wanted to watch the other channel. If you'd conducted a simple piece of research you might have discovered the film on BBC 2 that the whole family could have enjoyed together. Compromise need not always involve sacrifice; more often it requires a willingness to recognize acceptable alternatives.

However, I should warn you against the danger of placing too much dependence upon intelligence. It is, as I have said, a gift to be used and treasured, but you are – I make no apology for repeating this – you are mind, body and soul. Where intelligence falls short you must be happy to let emotion play its part. What you feel instinctively is as much a part of your nature as what you think. Add to that a strong faith which comes from a healthy spirit and you will be a whole man.

The reluctance to make faith's leap in the dark is the sloth of so-called atheists. It is easier – a soft option, you might say – to deny my existence than to wrestle with the theological problems and moral confusion that accompany belief. Equally though, the man who chooses a simple faith and neglects his intelligence is lazy, and prone to immaturity too. How often I have to return to this theme of growth. It is your reluctance to develop all sides of your personality which provokes me.

Still, given time, of which I at least have plenty, wholeness will come. Since your human time is limited, I can understand your impatience with so many councils and committees whose deliberations seem to come to nothing. In the vast expanse of my time, which is infinite, it would be even more difficult for you to detect progress towards me and the fulfilment I would eventually have you reach; but *I* see it, and I can afford to be patient.

You will fear that too much patience breeds complacency amongst humans. True, but you must take care to strike the right balance between thought and action. Ceaseless activity may look commendably industrious, but is often lacking in thought and purpose. You should not automatically rush in when you feel under pressure from other people who believe that their priorities should also be yours. The decision to wait or to take action I leave entirely in your hands, George. I insist on it. It is part of your growing up and – dare I say it again? – I want you to grow.

Finally, let me say something to remove the guilt you feel when your mind wanders in church. Sometimes the lack of concentration *is* laziness, there's no denying it. But there are times when it is the preacher's laziness that is to blame. He cannot expect you to listen if his prayers are vague and tedious through lack of preparation. You do better on such occasions to consider events and people of more specific and immediate need, and to offer your concern for them to me. I have noticed how regularly Maudie is in your prayers. To use your phrase, the end is very near now, but I am glad you remember her, especially since you are in a good position to effect some answer to the prayers you make for her. There is faith and works most usefully combined.

    With all my love,
    Yours sincerely,
    God.

... and the seventh deadly

Dear God,

Here's another confession! I suppose I should have taken notice long ago. You did warn me, but I thought I could get along quite well without your advice. Pride, I expect; the worst sin of all, you'll tell me.

I had to give Rosemary the shock and worry of finding me flaked out on the bathroom floor at half past midnight before I came to my senses. I'm feeling better now. The doctor came this morning and said there was nothing wrong that a few days rest wouldn't cure. Just a dizzy spell, he decided, brought on by too much rushing about; too many late nights and not enough time for relaxation. 'Have a week off,' he said; 'read some books, slow down and think about taking up golf when you're up and about again.'

So here I am, already much improved, thank you, and with time on my hands to write you a few lines. They'll have to manage without me for a few days at Waverley Advertising. I've discarded the silly notion that I was indispensable. I imagine I only told myself that to boost my ego when Edward Morris made me feel unwanted.

Still, he can go take a jump in the lake – (oops, sorry; but I won't cross it out. Once said, it's said, so I may as well admit that I thought it). But I've no need to worry myself about Edward Morris any more. This morning the post brought a letter of acceptance from Patterson's. So, with a new job to look forward to, and a doctor's certificate to justify staying away from Waverley for a few days, I'm in good spirits this morning, God, as I'm sure you know. You'll be able to hear my heart singing in spite of the cut in salary; after all, there's still the likelihood of Rosemary getting a little job. Between us, we shouldn't be much worse off. Patterson's is not so far into the city either, so I may even make a saving on petrol. Every little helps. I've also thought that in a year or two we might even move into the city and dispose of the car all together. With the money saved on the Road Fund licence, repairs and running costs, to say nothing of the hefty insurance premiums, we'd be rich. On the two salaries we might even buy a less cramped house than we've got at the moment; four or five bedrooms, room to move and breathe. There are some very imposing properties in the Barclay Park area. That would put Edward Morris in the shade, wouldn't it? If we wanted a car for holidays or trips to Northants to see our parents we could always hire one; something gleaming and new instead of our disintegrating antique.

It's amazing how simple it would all be. Of course, I may be counting chickens. . . . But better to be optimistic than down in the mouth.

I can hardly believe the sense of relief that's come with

this letter of acceptance. I suppose I'd run out of steam at Waverley. I can afford to admit it now. Patterson's will be a new start. You were right to insist that I went on struggling and hoping. It all seems worth while now. I've fought my way through and the feeling of achievement is terrific, like a tremendous vote of confidence. Thanks.

I've realized that you simply wanted me to prove to myself that I could do it if I persisted long enough; that I did have the ability in spite of my doubts – and the courage! That puzzles me a bit actually. Now I've done what you advised I can't help feeling just a little proud of myself. It was *my* experience and knowledge that got me the job, after all; it was *me* answering the questions at the interview, and I do *know* how to do a good job. Yet pride is labelled the deadliest sin of the seven. Is it really? Am I wrong to be proud of my achievements? Is it a sin to take pride in performing a task with skill and craftsmanship? I've always aimed high, determined to give nothing but the best quality service to the firm's clients, and frequently I've felt that glow of satisfaction which accompanies success. It can't be wrong, can it? To use another word for it instead of pride would surely only be playing with words. And I've a father's natural pride in David and Sara when they gain good exam. results at school or win certificates and prizes for swimming or music. I can't believe there's any sin in that. Perhaps you'll define pride for me when you write back. I can't help but think it's rather a slippery customer.

Must stop for a few minutes. Rosemary has just brought in the mid-morning coffee, all set out beautifully on a tray with the biscuits on a plate. I'd have just tucked them in the saucer, and then made them soggy by spilling the coffee over them on the way in! I sometimes think she likes me to be ill so that she can look after me. She does it so splendidly. Thanks for that too.

Coffee-break over. Rosemary brought the not unexpected

news that Maudie died at ten past two this morning. I was sorry that this enforced go-slow you've made me endure prevented me from visiting her at the weekend. She seems to have mellowed considerably, even over the few months that I've known her, and I quite enjoyed going to see her, listening and sharing her past. Perhaps it was the nearness of death that prompted her to try and make up for lost time. Is that possible, God? I've heard of death-bed repentances; people who'd spent their lives denying you and ridiculing religion, who changed their minds at the last minute. I suppose you can afford to swallow your pride when you're not going to be around to hear what people say about you. Not that Maudie was an unbeliever. As you know, she attended the local chapel quite regularly, until her illness made her too frail to make the journey. Yet the village would have judged her Christianity to have lacked warmth and tolerance. There seemed to be a kind of dogged observance about it, mixed, I always felt, with a sad longing for the 'good old days' when the chapel used to be packed to the doors.

I suppose the increasing sense of loneliness that accompanied her old age was bound to have her searching the past for days when the fellowship was richer and life had meaning because she was young enough to anticipate a lively future full of hope and promise. What's left, God, when you're eighty-four and dying of cancer?

I sometimes wonder how I shall face old age and death, assuming, perhaps quite mistakenly, that I shall live to be at least as old as Maudie, which will give me the opportunity to reflect upon it. What must it be like for those who are struck down swiftly and suddenly in a car crash or by a sniper's deadly bullet in the streets of Belfast? Lifted with a sharp jerk out of this life and (so you've always taught me to believe) into another, do they have pause for thought and, if necessary, repentance?

There's another question, God. Won't you ever leave my mind alone? *Is* it you, though? Now *there's* a question. *Is* it you that teaches me to believe in life after death, or is it simply human tradition? Is it pride at work again, breeding a reluctance to let go of my beliefs as effectively as it prevents the unbeliever from believing? You allow us to believe that truth is absolute, that we can contain it within a set of doctrines and obtain the salvation they promise by adhering strictly to them. Yet I wonder and question unceasingly, never certain whether it's pride endeavouring to undermine God-given teaching, or you stirring my intellect to continually poke holes in man-made assumptions.

There are, of course, some things that I accept without question. Whatever the means by which you did it I am ready to accept that you are the mind behind the creation of the universe, and amazed that my small part in it seems to be of some significance to you. I don't have to quarrel with those we call Fundamentalists, when it's so evident that we agree on basics. You made the world, and whether you took six days or six million years I regard as neither here nor there. But every so often I find myself wondering if the Fundamentalists might be right after all. In your whole scheme of things, I dare say it'll turn out not to matter in the least, but it's certainly a matter for debate amongst Christians. Not that I've ever known anyone go away convinced by the arguments of the others. Each prefers to cling stubbornly to his own version of the truth.

You know what I'm leading up to, don't you? I've been immersed in the Christian tradition, and brought up to think of Jesus as the only means of salvation—whatever that means. There I go again – heckling for change because the old-fashioned language doesn't meet with my approval. Who am I to make such demands?

Anyway, you tell me. Is Jesus unique? Am I to seek to understand and follow him alone, and reject the possibility of truth existing in the holy books and rituals of other religions? Are you so small, that the whole truth about you can be contained in the edited sayings of ancient writers and prophets of the Old Testament, and encapsulated in the life of Jesus – what little we know of it?

Hell's bells! If you're such an exclusive club, I'm not sure I want to belong! I'll find a way to keep in touch with you that suits me. You won't object, surely, as long as I'm aiming in the right direction? Or is that pride again; me wanting my own pig-headed way?

If there were more precise directions, God, there wouldn't be the danger of individuals asserting themselves. No wonder there are so many different denominations. Look at all the sects that exist beneath the umbrella of Christianity, to say nothing of the various major world religions and their myriad off-shoots. Variety may be the spice of life but it hardly makes for healthy religion, does it? It only makes for argument and opens the churches to criticism from those who've no patience with religion at all.

Of course, it's quite conceivable that the unbelievers are right. Perhaps I've been following a false trail all these years. Were it not for pride I might be willing to relinquish all the beliefs I hold. Tell me, are you real, or are you simply a figment of my imagination? Is it pride that deceives me into clinging to an illusion rather than lose face by admitting that my whole life up to this point has been attached to a huge lie?

Oh, God! If humility is the opposite of pride, and you commend the humility that admits to the possibility of being wrong, I could end up admitting that I've been mistaken about *you*.

But you've always been my security in this uncertain world. Does absence of pride mean losing my hold on you? What a dilemma! I must be more ill than I thought. I'll finish now and try to get some sleep.

Write soon,
Yours in desperation,
George

Dear George,

I'm really pleased for you. The new job at Patterson's will provide the motivation you need and restore your confidence. You had been so long at Waverley you had begun to think you knew it all, yet you couldn't withstand the criticism that led to self-doubt. You resented Edward Morris, not because his ideas were necessarily any better than your own, but because his alternative point of view made you question your own. You should have realized that this was only good and healthy for you, though, I admit, I didn't expect you to enjoy it at the time. Perhaps you'll accept its worth now that you've had some time to reflect upon it.

The stubborn resistance you put up, and the mental and emotional struggle that followed, were early symptoms of the dilemma you gave expression to at the end of your last letter. I couldn't help smiling as I observed you, rattling your beliefs like a bag of old tools that you had used and trusted for years, fancying that you had suddenly discovered previously unnoticed spots of rust, and flaws in the metal.

What is really interesting is that you had evidently started out to write to me about pride, and finished up in a turmoil of intellectual argument and confusion, bordering most dangerously on loss of faith. It only goes to show how deadly a sin pride is. It creeps up on you without your knowing. Indeed, the worst aspect of it is that you tend to notice pride only when you think you've identified it in others. You hardly ever notice it in yourself. You're quite right; it is a slippery customer.

You wrote to me first about Maudie. The whole batch of letters, you said, was prompted by that glass of pale ale she felt so guilty about. You made that 'clever' remark about the

people with starched collars and faces to match. There you are! In one supercilious phrase you belittled them, and the principles for which they stood. They were – and their descendants still are – good people. It is pride that persuades you to set up your own standards as the norm. Just think about that, George. Who are *you*?

And don't write to me about righteous indignation when you only use it to defend your own unexamined point of view. It's no excuse at all to say, 'I know I'm not perfect, but . . .'. How dare you assume that admitting your faults gives you the right to pick fault with others? Awareness of your own failings should prompt you to forgive those who share the lot of human weakness with you.

Pride even makes your gratitude worthless. You find it hard to accept help from someone you don't much like. When Edward Morris gave your name to Eastward TV and it resulted in some fine fat fees for acting as adviser to that series of programmes, all you could say, rather grudgingly was, 'Who would have thought Edward Morris, of all people, would have given me the chance...'. Really, George! I'm ashamed of you. Real thanksgiving has no place for condescension.

I have also noticed your habit of belittling your own talents, and appearing to squirm with embarrassment when a word of praise has contradicted you. Yet how you have inwardly revelled in it! If you would only accept that I have given you a part to play in my world, and be content to play it *with me*, not on your own, then you would have no worries over loss of confidence.

And how you love to play with words, George! It's quite understandable. You think of yourself as a writer, now that Eastward have accepted a number of your scripts. Words fascinate you, but you must beware of communicating false-hood instead of truth simply because the sound of the lies delights the ear. You have more than once written a sentence or two that sound most commendably humble. On the surface the words appear to ring true, but *I* am not deceived by your eloquence, George. In addition to humility, honesty and sincerity are enemies of pride.

You quite boldly declared in another letter, when you were writing about intoxicating drinks, that *you* knew when you'd had enough; yet you exceeded the limit when you went out to lunch with Eastward TV, almost fatally, both for you and the bus driver, who still shudders with horror and dis-belief every time he remembers the incident.

You even had the effrontery to suggest that sin was only a sin if it harmed someone else. You know nothing at all about it, do you? It is pride that wants you to think you can be safe and self-contained. But sin, whether it immediately harms others or not, makes a difference to the kind of person *you* are, and however hard you try, you cannot keep yourself completely to yourself. Do that, and you deprive the world of the useful things you are capable of giving to it, denying others the gifts that I would extend to them through you. That is selfishness. Equally, you would deprive yourself of the satisfaction you obtain when serving others meets with a warm response, and the pleasure of fulfilment that comes with the completion of another TV script.

If mention of that should worry you, if taking pleasure in personal achievement strikes you as a form of pride which ought to be avoided, think again. If your achievement is appropriate to the talents I have given you, then that is as it should be. You may freely take pleasure in the results. Only if you assume a superior attitude over someone who does not possess the same talents should you sense that pride is on the move again.

Be on your guard all the time, George. Be sensitive. Be continually self-critical. Self-examination is the discipline of true creativity, and should extend, not inhibit your growth. Didn't you prune the apple tree last autumn and witness, this summer, the improved shape, the increased yield, and an altogether healthier tree?

Pride, on the other hand, prevents maturity, because it is unwilling to open its heart and mind to all that life has to offer. The rich variety of experience from which you can learn and grow is cut off by pride which is frightened of change, blind to new truth, unwilling to trust anyone else, least of all me; for you do understand, don't you, George, that it is through trusting others that you declare your faith in me? Pride prefers to play safe, rejecting alternative points of view, believing in its own self-sufficiency, admitting no possibility of guilt or blame, and constantly seeking to justify its own position.

Pride is the most evil perpetrator of imbalance, turning courage into false heroics, self-confidence into arrogance. It pretends to offer certainty in an uncertain world, when its total dependence upon itself renders it most vulnerable. Pride, as you will often have heard, precedes many a fall. Yours took a tumble in the bathroom, you'll remember.

The confusion to which you came at the end of your letter was pride doing its utmost to convince you that you can rely upon your own intelligence, when the only sure way out of your dilemma is to have faith in me. You cannot work out your own salvation, save with fear and trembling. Not that I would have you discard your intelligence entirely. Intelligence and faith are both seed-beds of growth. Pride not only stunts personal growth but discourages the blossoming of others. Only total openness lends itself to a discovery of truth and freedom. Pride strives to maintain a fierce independence which common intelligence ought to recognize as futile and reject. Pride admits no choice and therefore destroys freedom. Pride prefers a closed shop, everything safe and secure in watertight compartments. It upholds a doctrine of irrefutable conclusions, accepting no truth other than unexamined 'truth' of its own making. Therefore it destroys truth.

Now, I know what you are thinking. I have begged the eternal question – 'What *is* truth?'

So I will tell you. Truth is a moment of decision. It is, for example, the moment when you put your application for the job at Patterson's in the post and committed yourself to the consequences of that action. It is the moment when you chose to take a cut in your salary, a reluctant yet courageous measure in pursuit of the happiness you anticipate finding in the new job. Intelligence has had its part to play. You have weighed up the advantages and disadvantages of the step you are taking, but you take it in faith; it is a risk.

Truth is real, not because it provides answers to unfathomable questions, but because of the tremendous demands it makes upon you to seek a solution which you believe will be acceptable to me. Truth is deliberate, active searching; a journey of the spirit through a physical world, attempting to make sense of it by making choices, and living life with a positive sense of direction. Truth is in having a point of view, but that in itself is not enough. Truth is not abstract. I repeat, it is real, and must be done that it may be seen to be real.

Your ceaseless questioning, George, you will be pleased to know, is an integral part of the activity described in the Fourth Gospel as 'doing the truth'. In these letters of yours – and mine too, since you choose to put words in my mouth – you have made a bold attempt to see with my eyes. I want you to know that all such attempts meet with my full approval, for by asking yourself how I would view things and, consequently deal with them, you have a good chance of acting justly and compassionately.

However, close as your words may come to reflecting my truth, you must not assume that they will remain true for ever. The best that can be said is that at the present stage of your development they are true. I am an unchanging God, but tomorrow a new experience may modify the truth you embrace today, or even cause you to discard it, for you will have learned a little more about me; even, perhaps, come to reflect in yourself, a closer resemblance to my image.

But I would warn you that to abandon pride in order to pursue understanding does not mean unquestioning obedience. That 'perfect submission' of which a few languishing hymn-writers wrote has little to do with faith. It sounds more like a soft option – 'Jump on God's wagon, let him do the driving'. What rubbish! I want men and women to make good use of their freedom; people who are bold enough to venture and risk making mistakes. Honest intent is all I require, and men and women with the courage of their convictions.

I know, to you, it will appear that I am deliberately inciting strife, but there is never any real growth without struggle, no progress without pain, no change without tears, no birth without death.

Well, George! Aren't I getting carried away! You see how your predicament has moved me! I *am* glad you wrote.

Let me now come to a particular question you posed. You have been brought up in a Christian tradition. Your church has led you to believe that Jesus is *The Truth*. According to the writings your church has preserved, Jesus himself, in the Gospel according to St John, describes himself as the Way, the Truth, and the Life.

You are quite right when you say this sounds exclusive. You do well to question whether this is pride at work again. There is certainly much truth to be found amongst the rituals and writings of other religions. Christianity is certainly unique, but it has no monopoly of truth. In saying that Jesus is *The Truth* the contributions that other religions have made to your spiritual journey, and that of many others, are not to be lightly or scornfully tossed aside.

What I will give you to think about is this: when in the Fourth Gospel Jesus is set forth as the Way, the Truth and the Life, the message was to people of the writer's own time and place. The words are not applicable to you in twentieth-century Great Britain without interpretation. Remember also what I said about the necessity for a point of view. If you prefer the word 'belief', then I will accept that, but for my sake, have one that is your very own; a second-hand faith, or one that's borrowed from somebody else is precious little use. If this starts you doubting, don't worry, just wrestle with them; but about Jesus I will say this one thing more, to help you.

His life and work were of a unique character. Through no one else has there been for me the opportunity within a human being to say as much about myself as I did through him. When your church teaches you to follow his example, it is not the same as saying that you should be like me. That would be impossible; but, in attempting to be like Jesus, you will be striving to be like me to the fullest extent that your human frame and earthly circumstances will allow.

What you have to aim at, George, is all that I will let you do and be if you put yourself completely into my hands. That's not a restrictive commitment, but a potentially fulfilling one. I hope that also explains why I consistently refuse to provide you with precise rules of conduct and belief. You do keep pestering me for them, thinking that they will give you security. Don't you see that a set of rigid rules, or a laid-down set of doctrines requiring strict obedience, would at once have you placing each other in order of merit. You would come to expect prizes for good behaviour; an open invitation to pride! Sadly, some of you view heaven in just such a fashion.

You know the rules that Jesus ascribed to, don't you? Love God, and love your neighbour. So vague, you say, that they're not a lot of help; but truly, anything more closely defined would restrict the good you do. Dedication always exceeds the minimum requirements, and you must beware, since this is so, of taking all credit for your recent success for yourself. I know that it was *your* voice, your *mind* that answered the questions in Patterson's personnel office. It was certainly the accumulated knowledge from your own experience that gave you confidence, but your experience is not something that you have gained in isolation. It is the influence of countless people with whom you have rubbed shoulders, had discussions, even merely passed the time of day, in the office, in the pub, down at the shops. And don't forget the love and support you have had from Rosemary, David and Sara, all through this crisis. You would have been lost and lonely without their patience and understanding.

You are part of something so much bigger than yourself, comprised of past history which has shaped your present, present experience that builds your future, and speculation about your future which prompts your actions here and now. Your character – so vital in persuading Patterson's that you were the man for the job – reflects the amazing variety of people, places and incidents that have made you what you are. It is through all these things that I work, George. Things past, things present, and things future all contribute to your personal growth.

Oh, George, how the very mention of pride fires my

tongue! But I have lectured you long enough. If you will but learn the lesson that your tumble in the bathroom should have taught you I know that you will then view independence with suspicion if it ever means rejecting an offer of help or advice. In trusting and accepting, you will become one with me and my creation, and pride will be conquered.

Accept too this final blow – though with some compensation, as you will discover. While I value all that you have done in my name, especially for Maudie, you are not indispensable, even to me. I tell you this because if anything is designed to work against pride, it is the knowledge that I can do perfectly well without you. I also share this secret with you because of your fascination with paradox. I may choose to make use of you in my work on earth or not; I may cause you to receive great fame by the standards of the world you live in, or I may choose for you an occupation which the world holds to be of no significance. The effect of this should be to lend you a fuller appreciation of the love that I have for you.

It was the writer of one of the psalms who put the question to me long ago – 'What is man that thou art mindful of him, and the son of man that thou dost care for him?' What indeed?

Who are *you*, George, that I should love you so? And yet I do, with all my heart.

Your friend,
God

. . . and a question of judgement

Dear George,

This is really no more than a long P.S., expanding a little the remarks I made at the end of my last letter, and commenting on the death of Maudie.

You will miss her, I know. Your own kindness, and her frailty, allowed her stern outer shell to be broken down, letting some of the real Maudie come through. She was well known for her sharp tongue; she had ruined many a good character by jumping to false conclusions about them, and cultivating rumours with no truth in them, but she was not spiteful or malicious.

You will want to know whether I intend some eternal

judgement for Maudie's failings now that she's dead. How lacking you are in perception, that you go on perpetuating the story of heaven and hell with such colourful imagery.

I have no kingdom of the kind you envisage, to which entrance is gained through a set of pearly gates leading to a palace of ivory and crystal with Roman pillars and marble floors, where white-robed angels sing alleluia forever, accompanying themselves on golden harps. I couldn't stand the din! Nor is there, alternatively, a lake of fire and brimstone prepared for the torture of evil-doers. I prefer silence to the weeping, wailing and gnashing of teeth you imagine awaits them.

You must not confuse your earthly values with mine, expecting rewards for the good and punishments for the bad. That is not the truth I urge you to seek, that is favouritism or vindictiveness. Truth is the action that I take to achieve redemption. I know! That's one of those old-fashioned religious terms that makes your flesh creep, so let me explain.

You have earthly standards for justice, and you assume that mine are the same. That is a mistake. You speak of fairness and of people receiving their just deserts. My justice is not like that. I am more concerned with needs than with earnings. Your fascination with paradox should have prepared you for the truth that I seek hardest for those who are furthest from me; yet that is hardly paradox, you ought rather to call it common sense.

I love what I have created. Because I love you I have given you freedom. When that freedom is abused, I am hurt, and most anxious that the one who has hurt me so, should turn and love me again, but freely, without coercion or threat of punishment.

If that to you seems careless, it is because the smallness of your faith breeds caution. It is also because you overlook the extent to which those who commit sins frequently bring about consequences which are punishment enough in themselves. Maudie's loneliness was evidence of this, and your tumble in the bathroom too. Would you have me heap more upon these?

I must also make it clear to you that there is a distinction to be made between sins and *Sin*. Sins are actions, self-evident crimes against me and humanity. *Sin* is the rotten core from which such actions grow. Sins are no more than irritating blisters on the skin, while *Sin* is deep down inside, eating away at the soul. Sins are forgivable, even though their consequences may have repercussions long after the sinner has been forgiven. To forgive is not to forget, it is to remember without hate. Nevertheless, the actions are some indication of how far sin has displaced me in people's hearts.

You, as a Christian, believe in the Word made flesh, acknowledging that I have a dwelling place in you. Therefore what you do or say in your dealings with others passes judgement on the God who dwells in them, and presumes to be spoken by the God in you. An awesome responsibility for you, George! How important it is, then, to proceed always with sensitivity and caution, not least because you cannot always be certain what your sins are. I cannot help smiling at the guilt which sometimes accompanies a break with tradition or a change of habit, or the words you have spoken with good intent that curiously managed to give offence.

I openly confess that I have not given you an easy world to live in. Mostly, your problem is that you see the world as though it were all there is, but I see the whole, of which your world is only a minute part. In spite of this, you judge other people when you are not even capable of judging yourselves. You see what you believe to be sins committed by others, but you are quite unaware of the circumstances which provoked them; certainly you are in no position to know whether the actions were sins, regretted as soon as performed, or the consequence of deep-rooted *Sin* – that deliberate turning away from me. Get this thing clear – I do not turn away from you, ever.

I know you, George, as I knew and still know Maudie. I do not judge in ignorance. I know the state of your mind and emotions, the pressures of work, family and other commitments which cause you to do things of which you are at once ashamed. I know whether a life is striving towards me, or away from me, and I make my judgements in that knowledge.

My judgement is not fair or impartial by human standards. The righteous man, conceited enough to think that he is entitled to a greater reward than the sinner is in for a shock. Read again the story of Jesus, George, of his commitment to life and people, how his actions matched his words, how he spoke, performed, and therefore *was* The Truth.

I have said already that it was through him that I was enabled to say more about myself than through any other human being, either before or since. Has the reckless extravagance of his death not taught you that I am considerably biased (in your terms) in favour of the sinner? My kind of love is never fair, because it always gives more than it gets.

The honest sinner is often more closely bound to me by his shame and sense of failure than the righteous man by his good works and apparent success.

I wish you well in your new beginning, George. Don't forget to write.

Always yours,
God